Franciscans and Liturgical Life

Let Us Praise, Adore and Give Thanks

Washington Theological Union
Symposium Papers
2006

©The Franciscan Institute
St. Bonaventure University
St. Bonaventure, NY 14778
2006

CFIT/ESC-OFM Series
Number 6

All rights reserved.
No part of this book may be reproduced or transmitted
in any form or by any means, electronic or mechanical,
without permission in writing from the publisher.

The articles in this book were originally presented
at a symposium sponsored by the Franciscan Center
at Washington Theological Union, Washington, DC,
May 26-28, 2006.

This publication is the sixth in a series of documents
resulting from the work of the
Commission on the Franciscan Intellectual Tradition of the
English-speaking Conference of the
Order of Friars Minor.
(CFIT/ESC-OFM)

Cover design: Jennifer L. Davis

ISBN: 978-157659-1413

Library of Congress Control Number
2006940790

Printed and bound in the United States of America

BookMasters, Inc.
Ashland, Ohio

TABLE OF CONTENTS

Abbreviations vi

Preface
    Ilia Delio, O.S.F. ix

Chapter One
    Is Liturgy the Heart of the Church Today?
    Catherine Dooley, O.P. 1

Chapter Two
    Sacramentality and Franciscan Worship
    Judith Kubicki, O.S.F. 11

Chapter Three
    Franciscan Theology of the Eucharist:
    Does It Inform Our Lives?
    James Sabak, O.F.M. 27

Chapter Four
    Liturgy of the Hours
    and the Rhythm of Franciscan Life
    William Cieslak, O.F.M., Cap. 51

Chapter Five
    Franciscan Devotionalism
    and Postmodern Culture
    Daniel Grigassy, O.F.M. 71

About the Authors 91

ABBREVIATIONS

Writings of Saint Francis

Adm	The Admonitions
BlL	A Blessing for Brother Leo
CtC	The Canticle of the Creatures
CtExh	The Canticle of Exhortation
LtAnt	A Letter to Brother Anthony of Padua
1LtCl	First Letter to the Clergy (Early Edition)
2LtCl	Second Letter to the Clergy (Later Edition)
1LtCus	The First Letter to the Custodians
2LtCus	The Second Letter to the Custodians
1LtF	The First Letter to the Faithful
2LtF	The Second Letter to the Faithful
LtL	A Letter to Brother Leo
LtMin	A Letter to a Minister
LtOrd	A Letter to the Entire Order
LtR	A Letter to Rulers of the Peoples
ExhP	Exhortation to the Praise of God
PrOF	A Prayer Inspired by the Our Father
PrsG	The Praises of God
OfP	The Office of the Passion
PrCr	The Prayer before the Crucifix
ER	The Earlier Rule (Regula non bullata)
LR	The Later Rule (Regula bullata)
RH	A Rule for Hermitages
SalBVM	A Salutation of the Blessed Virgin Mary
SalV	A Salutation of Virtues
Test	The Testament
TPJ	True and Perfect Joy

Early Biographical Sources

1C	The Life of Saint Francis by Thomas of Celano
2C	The Remembrance of the Desire of a Soul
LJS	The Life of Saint Francis by Julian of Speyer

1MP	The Mirror of Perfection (Smaller Version)
2MP	The Mirror of Perfection (Larger Version)
ScEx	The Sacred Exchange between Saint Francis and Lady Poverty
AP	The Anonymous of Perugia
L3C	The Legend of the Three Companions
AC	The Assisi Compilation
LMj	The Major Legend by Bonaventure

Francis of Assisi: Early Documents, ed. Regis Armstrong, Wayne Hellmann, William Short, three volumes (New York: New City Press, 1999, 2000, 2001)

PREFACE

About two years before he died, Francis of Assisi composed his *Canticle of the Creatures*. Although he was very ill, blind, and near death, this light-filled hymn emerged from his inner depths as a song of praise and glory resounding throughout the whole creation. The *Canticle*, in a sense, recapitulated the life of Francis, a life of prayer, praise and adoration to the living God of overflowing love. His fidelity to the Liturgy of the Hours, his sacramental view of creation and his Christ-centeredness, all reflected in the *Canticle,* remind us that Francis's life was, at its core, a liturgical life.

Although liturgy may have been at the heart of Francis, Franciscans have paid little attention to the development of a Franciscan liturgical life and the import of this life for ministry. Daniel Grigassy points out in this volume that, while Franciscans should be at the forefront of liturgy and mission, others for whom liturgy is less characteristic, such as the Jesuits, have taken the lead. This lacuna raises several questions. How does liturgical life shape Franciscan life? Is there a "Franciscan" liturgical life and, if so, what is it?

These questions are particularly important at a moment in history when the whole Franciscan intellectual tradition is under renewed consideration. We here at the Franciscan Center of the Washington Theological Union make our contribution to this renewal by engaging the Franciscan tradition with questions of contemporary significance. Since the import of liturgy on the shape of Franciscan life has received little attention, we gathered together experts in the field of liturgy, primarily Franciscans, to discuss the meaning of Franciscan liturgical life.

Although the papers contained in this volume have a particular focus on the intersection between liturgical life and Franciscan life, we begin with the more general question, is liturgy at the heart of the Church today? Catherine Dooley, a Dominican Sister who teaches liturgy and catechetics at Catholic University of America, addresses this question with breadth and depth in her paper. Highlighting the present decline in church attendance, she offers a brief historical background to the nature of liturgy, stressing the importance of mystagogy for participation in liturgy as a way of life. If liturgy is to be at the heart of the Church, she claims, ongoing catechesis as a way of deepening one's participation in the mysteries of the faith is necessary.

Judith Kubicki, a Felician Sister who teaches sacramental and liturgical theology at Fordham University, leads us into Franciscan liturgical life through a lucid and substantive discussion of Franciscan sacramentality and worship. Noting the polyvalent meaning of symbol and its relation to sacrament, she underscores creation's innate "sacramentality" and the importance of bodiliness in communicating God's presence to the world. Imagination is at the heart of sacramentality, Kubicki claims, and she calls us to renew our sacramental imagination.

James Sabak, a Friar Minor of the Holy Name Province, is a doctoral student at the Catholic University of America, concentrating in the area of liturgy. In his timely yet challenging topic on the relationship between the Eucharist and Franciscan life, he gives us both a historical and a contemporary treatment. Through a brief analysis of the Eucharist in its medieval, social and liturgical contexts, he draws out aspects of a Franciscan Eucharistic theology that can help shape our life today. Sabak also raises some challenges with regard to the unifying significance of the Eucharist and the separations that continue to exist in the First Order of Friars Minor.

William Cieslak, a Capuchin friar and past president of the Franciscan School of Theology at Berkeley, offers a succinct but comprehensive treatment of the centrality of the Liturgy of the Hours for Franciscan life. Cieslak describes "Franciscanism" as a spirituality intended for every circumstance of life and highlights the distinctiveness of Franciscan prayer as "attitude over form" and "heart over mind." Reminding us of Francis's creativity and freedom in reciting the psalms, he calls us to develop a Franciscan attitude toward praying the Liturgy of the Hours that follows the free and creative spirit of Francis.

Finally, Daniel Grigassy, former professor of Word and Worship at Washington Theological Union and also a friar of Holy Name Province, provides a substantive yet humorous discussion of Franciscan devotions and postmodern culture. Noting the obscurity of the term "postmodern" and its variants, "paramodern" and "transmodern," he locates a hermeneutic of postmodern culture in the distinction between "idol" (a projection of the subject onto the object) and "icon" (a diaphanous light that shines through from one subject to another). He then highlights several distinct Franciscan devotions that he first learned as a "seraphic" seminarian in the '60s, such as the Transitus and Franciscan Crown, and describes how they have been distorted over time to suit the needs of the pious. Essentially, he advocates the practice of these devotions to enhance our contemporary spiritual life, suggesting that they could be especially helpful to a postmodern culture that seeks meaningful signs and symbols. However, he warns, we must continue to beware of turning iconic devotions into idols for spiritual consumption.

As these papers on Franciscan liturgical life were presented this past May, one could not help but catch the contagious virus of energy that permeated the air. Each topic of liturgical life touched the core of the Franciscan spirit, and one could hear whispered among the participants: "Are not our hearts burning within us?" May the fire of the Spirit illuminating this volume of excellent scholarship ignite within its readers a creative spirit of prayer so that our lives may be lifted up in praise, adoration and thanksgiving to a God of generous love and great humility.

Ilia Delio, O.S.F.
Director of the Franciscan Center
Washington Theological Union
September 2006

CHAPTER ONE

IS LITURGY THE HEART OF THE CHURCH TODAY?

Catherine Dooley, O.P.

Is liturgy the heart of the Church today? This is an interesting question and one that could be answered in many different ways depending perhaps on how one understands the meaning of the key words—liturgy and Church.

A Statistical View

If we understand the Church as an organization, some current sociological research indicates that perhaps the answer to the question would not be entirely positive. Although liturgy encompasses more than the Sunday celebration of the Eucharist, Mass attendance is often an indicator of the importance of liturgy. For example, from 2000 to 2004, the Center for Applied Research in the Apostolate (CARA) conducted a series of ten national random-sample telephone polls on Catholic life in the United States.[1] One of the questions was: "Aside from weddings and funerals, about how often do you attend Mass?" The results in 2004 estimated that about forty percent of Catholics attend Sunday Mass every week. The CARA report explains the long-term decline in Catholic Mass attendance in terms of a generational change. The older generation consistently attends Mass more frequently than the Vatican II age group (b. 1943-1960) or the post-Vatican II group (b. 1960 to present); but as this older generation dies, the percentage will also decline.

Other statistics show that church membership has more than doubled in size in the past half century. This increase is primarily due to

---

[1] The Center for Applied Research in the Apostolate, "Self-reported Mass Attendance of U.S. Catholics Unchanged during Last Five Years (Washington, DC: Georgetown University, 2004). (Internet: http://cara.georgetown.edu/AttendPR.pdf)

the influx of immigrant populations that are traditionally Catholic. Recent articles in the *Washington Post* indicate, however, that many of these are joining evangelical groups, and some have converted to Islam. Studies also show that the rate of infant baptism has steadily fallen (or as the title of an article in *USA Today* described it: "Rite of Baptism Trickles Away"[2]). Other factors with regard to the Eucharist are an increase in the number of so-called priestless parishes, a decline in the number of seminarians and greater reliance on international priests to staff parishes.

More Than an Organization

If statistics are an indicator of the health and stability of an organization, then the view of the Church as an organization is fairly bleak. The Second Vatican Council reminds us, however, that the Church is more than an organization—it is a mystery of God's love, the People of God, a pilgrim Church, a sacrament for the world, a servant Church, a praying Church, a hierarchical Church, a communion and the Body of Christ. In this broader context, the *Constitution on the Sacred Liturgy* (SC) emphatically affirms the centrality of liturgy in the life of the Church, stating that the work of our redemption takes place through the liturgy especially in the divine sacrifice of the Eucharist. "It is through the liturgy especially that the faithful are enabled to express in their lives and manifest to others the mystery of Christ and real nature of the true Church" (SC, no. 2). In Chapter 1, the *Constitution* makes the bold statement: "The liturgy is the summit toward which the activity of the Church is directed; it is also the source from which all its power flows" (SC 10).[3] Obviously, the Vatican Council documents affirmed liturgy as the heart of the Church. Why is this not obvious to all who are Catholic Christians?

History and Catechesis as Key

Perhaps one reason lies in history and another in the failure to provide the kind of catechesis called for in the Vatican documents. Historically speaking, there is a certain sense in which liturgical studies/liturgical

---

[2] 12 April 2006.

[3] Austin Flannery, ed. *The Basic Sixteen Documents Vatican Council II* (Northport, NY: Costello Publishing Company, 1996.)

theology is just coming of age and returning to the principles that were prevalent in the early Church. In recent church documents, there is more and more reference to the early Church, a return to the so-called "golden age" of the catechumenate. For example, the *General Directory for Catechesis*, published in 1997, states that the baptismal catechumenate is a model for all catechesis. In support of this assertion, the *Directory* rarely refers to the *Rite of Christian Initiation* but rather to fourth- and fifth-century bishops like Cyril of Jerusalem, Ambrose, John Chrysostom, Theodore and Augustine. The catechesis of these church leaders was based on the experience of their hearers, the meaning of the liturgical actions and the prayer texts in light of the Scriptures. Their approach can be summed up in the axiom, *legem credendi lex statuat supplicandi*,[4] attributed to Prosper of Aquitaine, a contemporary of St. Augustine. (Today we have shortened the saying to *lex orandi lex credendi*, often adding *lex vivendi*). These early bishops believed that prayer (*lex orandi*), particularly liturgical prayer, has a fundamental role in shaping what we believe (*lex credendi*) and, consequently, how we live out the Gospel (*lex vivendi*). For these great preachers and teachers, the words, the prayers, the symbols and the rituals were all of a piece.

Underlying their organic approach to preaching and catechesis was the sacramental principle that all created reality is capable of manifesting God. Their understanding of sacrament was based on a way of viewing reality that *sees* God in the visible, the tangible, the finite, the historical, because all things have the possibility of revealing God. The early bishops preached that God's self-revelation and communication with humankind takes place through the mediation of material elements, people, events, the works of creation and human culture. (The *Catechism of the Catholic Church* also adds other religions, no. 1149). All of these signs and symbols are integrated into the sacraments of the Church, through which the Holy Spirit accomplishes the work of our redemption.

In the early church councils, the exploration of the meaning of theological doctrines such as the mystery of the Trinity or the divinity of Jesus was influenced by how doctrines were articulated and cel-

---

[4] For a comprehensive development of the concept, see Kevin Irwin, "Lex Orandi, Lex Credendi—Origins and Meaning: State of the Question," *Liturgical Ministry*, 11 (Spring 2002), 57-69.

ebrated in the Church's liturgy. Liturgy as a theological source was obvious in the preaching and teaching of early church leaders. They preached and catechized on the sacraments from the Scriptures in the context of the liturgy with a view to living the Christian life. Their sermons were thoroughly biblical and were extended by liturgical rituals, the same actions that we have today in the *Order of Christian Initiation:* the signing of the cross, the anointing with oil, exorcisms, the presentation and recitation of the Creed and the Our Father. The liturgical actions were considered catechesis. We find an example of this around the year 500, when John the Deacon explains about the rite known as a scrutiny. He says this rite is nothing less than a formal act of catechesis done now no longer apart from the community but with its participation and in its solemn presence. The Church's minister lays hands on the heads of the catechumens that they may know who they are and who they will be.[5]

Catechumens were not only prepared for the event of the sacrament, but after they were baptized, there was a period of time called mystagogy, during which the bishops assisted the newly baptized to reflect on the mysteries that had just been celebrated. This process led the neophytes to recall all they had experienced, enabled them to integrate their experience with their instruction and helped them to realize who they were and who they were called to be.

A Disconnect between Liturgy and Theology

From the eighth to the sixteenth centuries, Patristic integration gradually diminished due to a variety of political, social and religious factors. Liturgical unity became liturgical uniformity, and the active participation of the people was reduced to passivity. With the rise of the universities, questions about sacraments became detached from worship. The scholastics, for example, focused on the differentiation of the sacraments, their number, their institution, and the matter and form of each. The Council of Trent (1565), in its effort to refute the reformers and correct existing abuses, completed the separation between sacraments and liturgy. The Council was concerned with rubrics, so much so that these rubrics were printed in the Roman Missal alongside the prayers. Little by little, liturgy became more and more equated with the external performance of the Church's rites.

---

[5] E. C. Whitaker, ed., *Documents of the Baptismal Liturgy* (London: SPCK, 1960), 145.

Sacramental theology was incorporated into manuals of dogmatic theology that in general paid little attention to the rites as a theological source. The result was a rather legalistic understanding of liturgy. Liturgical texts in theological discourse were generally used as proof texts as were scriptural references.

The 1917 Code of Canon Law placed sacraments under *"De Rebus"* ("of things"). In the universities, sacraments were generally taught in the context of moral theology, because sacraments were seen as a means of living a moral life. Liturgical courses, designed primarily for seminarians, were looked upon almost as "how to" courses.

A New Movement in Our Times

Both before and after the Second Vatican Council, however, theologians and contemporary church documents began to give more attention to the relationship between liturgy and theology, renewing appreciation for the whole liturgy as an enacted set of rites and symbolic acts that needed to be interpreted theologically and pastorally.

The 1983 Code of Canon Law considers sacraments under the broad umbrella of liturgy in the section on "The Office of Sanctifying in the Church," the section of the Code that governs the liturgical life and celebration of the Latin rite. This section is grounded in the *Constitution on the Sacred Liturgy* and offers a profound understanding of sacraments as expressing and manifesting the mystery of Christ and the real nature of the true Church.

One of the outstanding contributions of the *Catechism of the Catholic Church* (CCC) is the placement of the sacraments within the context of liturgy. This is unique in a catechism genre. The CCC is the first catechism to use the terminology of liturgical catechesis (no. 1074), stating that the liturgy is the privileged place for catechizing the people of God. The aim of liturgical catechesis is "to initiate people into the mystery of Christ by proceeding from the visible to the invisible, from the sign to the thing signified, from the sacraments to the mystery" (no. 1075).

Today, we are beginning to come full circle. The restorations mandated by Vatican II, the Code of Canon Law, the *Catechism*, the writings of liturgical theologians and certainly the restoration of the catechumenate (RCIA) have contributed greatly to an awareness that liturgy is the heart of the Church. The revisions have not only been about the rituals but about a change in the Church's self-understanding, offering a new vision of what it means to be Church and what "full, conscious, active participation" means. It is important now not to give old explanations to the new rites, nor revert to a certain "rubricism" or individualism, such as the Council of Trent fostered in its efforts at clarity.

Perhaps the thing most neglected in the past forty years was thoughtful, sustained catechesis and preaching on the liturgy as called for by the *Constitution on the Sacred Liturgy*. If a primary goal of the reform is the full, conscious and active participation of all the people, then it is necessary to learn the language of sign and symbol, a language that is accompanied and given life by the Word of God and the response of faith. The liturgy, whose language is sign and symbol, words and actions, singing and music, images and icons, must be intelligible to those who participate in it.

The early mystagogues give us a paradigm. Liturgical catechesis is an integrated process rooted in Scripture and framed by the liturgical seasons and feasts. It reflects on the rites and symbols in the context of the particular community celebrating. The content of catechesis and preaching includes reflection not only on the Scriptures but also on ritual texts, symbols and symbolic actions, and the theological and historical backgrounds that uncover and disclose the meaning of the liturgy for our lives. The "method" of catechesis is participation in word and symbol. It is the celebrating itself that shapes attitudes and outlooks and transforms actions.

Imagination as Power

The *Constitution on the Sacred Liturgy* (33) states: "Although the liturgy is above all things the worship of the divine majesty, it also contains rich instruction for the faithful." The instruction is not so much didactic as it is holistic. Liturgical catechesis depends upon the development of imagination. Imagination in this context is not illusion but rather, as St. Thomas writes, it is a power of the soul. He describes imagination as the storehouse of all that comes to us through the senses.[6] Out of this storehouse we draw ideas, words and possibilities that enable a personal integration of faith. Imagination has to do with the capacity to form images, images that are dependent upon past experience. Imagination allows us to participate in what we imagine by putting ourselves into another person's place or situation. Imagination allows us to see possibilities. It enables us to change and to be transformed.

---

[6] I q. 78 art. 4.

If this idea of imagination seems out of place with regard to liturgy or catechesis, we need only turn to Jesus, the master teacher. In his parables, he calls forth experience and memory. He tells the disciples about a situation that is familiar to them but which requires them to see different possibilities in the situation and then to make a decision. The disciples come to the insight that the story is not just about some farmer sowing seed, but it is about themselves. Imagination allows us to enter into the process of making meaning out of life. Imagination is integral to the sacramental principle, the process of "seeing God" in all created reality. The catechesis model offered by the early bishops has inspired contemporary documents, such as the *Rite of Christian Initiation,* to develop a conversion process for unbaptized adults and to underline the importance of mystagogy not only for those in the catechumenate but for all believers.

The Validity of Ancient Methodologies for Our Times

The methodology of the patristic teachers and preachers had three phases: preparation for, celebration of and reflection on. Each phase was directed to the living out of the Christian life and was seen as a whole process.

How is this methodology applicable today? I will try to illustrate a contemporary process of liturgical catechesis based on the patristic tradition. For the early mystagogues, the preparation phase was necessarily more didactic than the other phases of catechesis. The foundation of any catechesis starts with the celebrating assembly. Liturgical catechesis begins with the theology of the rite found in the introduction to the rite. In this introduction are also the principles of catechesis. What are the key principles? What is the purpose of the rite according to the introduction? What is the role of the minister and of the community in this rite? What images are used to describe the sacrament/rite in the introduction and in the prayer texts of the rite? What scripture texts are suggested? What images are central in the scripture readings and in the prayers? How do these images relate to the symbol/symbolic actions of the rite? How do these images relate to the life of the community? What liturgical season is being celebrated? This preparation phase is essential in order for the participants to develop a lexicon of images, rituals, symbols, gestures, music and sacred space so they might be open to the mystery of God within the liturgy.

The purpose of catechesis, then, is not to explain away the rites about to be celebrated but to help people enter with greater understanding into the mystery of Christ present among us. Liturgical catechesis, when done well, leads to well-celebrated rites. Ritual is meant to form the participants through repetition and through exploring the multiple meanings inherent in the ritual itself. Good liturgy is formative; poor liturgy is not.

The Rite of Penance as an Example

Using the *Rite of Penance* as an example, we discover that it is very rich and can be developed from a number of different aspects. It would seem odd to catechize on the sacrament of Penance thinking only in terms of confession of sin. Confession is just one aspect of the sacramental ritual. The words of contrition and forgiveness lead to a resolve to consider, decide and act in response to the gracious love of God revealed in Jesus Christ and given to us a hundredfold. Mystagogy is communal reflection, and the *Rite of Penance* emphasizes the ecclesial aspect of this sacrament.

One of the underlying themes in the *Rite of Penance* is its relationship to Baptism and Eucharist. In fact, the ritual states that the purpose of frequent celebration of the sacrament is to strive to perfect the grace of Baptism. Moreover, in order that it truly achieve its healing purpose, it should take root in the whole life of the faithful and be manifest in service of God and neighbor (RP, no. 7b). The Rite insists on the solidarity of people in both sin and grace. We are called to salvation not only as individuals but as a community. The Rite adds that it is important for Christians to help one another in the process of forgiveness and reconciliation so that "freed from sin by the grace of Christ they may work with all people of good will for justice and peace in the world" (RP, no. 5). Six of the eleven readings suggested for the *Rite of Individual Penance* propose that the sacrament is to free people for lives of generosity and service. Because the sacrament is a manifestation of God's love and forgiveness, Christians are called to look outward and forward in confidence and gratitude.

Catechesis on this sacrament would also include identifying the images in the rite, in the readings, or in any of the texts. One of the suggested readings for individual penitents is Luke 15:1-7. The Pharisees and Scribes are scandalized because Jesus welcomes sinners and eats with them. The reading includes the parable of the lost sheep, so the passage is replete with images. This great parable of forgiveness, however, is told at the table; and so, in the catechesis for the sacrament, we might simply look at two aspects of it—"welcome" and "eats with them." What is the experience of the listeners with regard to both "welcome" and "eats with them"? What do those images mean in terms of the particular culture or upbringing of the participants? What are other stories in the Gospels of welcome and eating?

People very easily understand that these images represent life, community, relationship, Eucharist, or Jesus himself as the Bread of Life. In the tapestry of all of these images and memories, what meaning is conveyed through the celebration of the sacrament of reconciliation? Insights are often very profound and enable people to focus on the action of God, God's mercy and God's steadfast love and on their own response of gratitude and love. The process of catechesis moves the reflection from the rite to personal experience to the community or society to the Scriptures and back to the rites. An essential question is always: "What does this ask of us?"

The liturgical actions of kneeling, making the sign of the cross and imposing hands are important to consider. In the past, the minister was told to raise his right hand over the penitent and make the sign of the cross. The ancient gesture of imposition of hands was unrecognizable. In fact, most people assumed the priest was raising his hand to bless the penitent. The imposition of hands has multiple meanings both in the Scriptures and in the sacramental rituals—blessing, invocation of the Holy Spirit, restoration to communion with the Church, investing with authority, healing, etc. In the *Rite of Penance*, the priest, through this gesture, calls upon the God of mercy to give pardon and peace.

Very often the celebration of reconciliation takes place during Lent. What does the season of the year contribute to the preparation? Lent has a focus on both Baptism and Penance (SC, 109). The charge to make the baptismal character of Lent more pronounced has been aided by the focus on the preparation of catechumens to be baptized at the Easter vigil.

The Importance of Mystagogy

The celebration of the rite is followed by mystagogy, reflection on the mysteries of what has been experienced. Mystagogy is the most important and the most neglected aspect of every sacrament. Cyril of Jerusalem catechized on the sacraments after they had been celebrated, because the neophytes would be more open to learning about what they had already experienced. He would ask them to remember the words and actions of the ritual in order to draw out the deepest levels of meaning. "Think what you saw; think what you said," Cyril would say to them. In this way, mystagogy brings together the individual and community experiences, the word of God, the received tradition and the liturgical season or feast within the context of the community. What were the individuals' experiences of the rite? What biblical images were evident to them? How did the prayers and readings relate to their life experiences? How did the readings/prayers call them to conversion? Catechesis opens up these symbols so the participants may see God present in their lives and respond to the demands of the Gospel.

Conclusion

Ritual prayer is constitutive of our identity as Christian people. The whole of the liturgy reminds us that we are one in Christ. In the liturgy we celebrate our identity as the People of God called to believe in the Triune God through this community of faith. The sacramental rites not only express our relationship to God and to one another but, in the power of the Spirit, they effect it. The formative power of liturgy comes through repetition and symbol (that which makes the reality present). The actions and prayers of the liturgy and the proclamation of the Scripture enliven the imagination to perceive new perspectives and new possibilities for one's life. Those who enter into the ritual experience a call to conversion and transformation.

Is the liturgy the heart of the Church? Perhaps we will only be able to give a resounding "Yes" to that question when we who are ministers become mystagogues.

CHAPTER TWO

SACRAMENTALITY AND FRANCISCAN WORSHIP[1]

Judith M. Kubicki, C.S.S.F.

Introduction

If ever there were a person who cultivated a sacramental view of life, it was Francis of Assisi. Everywhere he looked, Francis perceived God's presence: in the beauty of creation, in the smallest of God's creatures, in the silence of contemplative prayer. His devotion to the humanity of Christ through his celebration of the crèche at Greccio and the Stations of the Cross, or his composing the ecstatic *Canticle of the Sun*—all of these express a sacramental worldview that saw and heard God's presence in all aspects of creation. Francis intuitively grasped a core belief of Christianity: that God uses simple elements of ordinary, everyday life to cultivate a deep and abiding relationship of love with humanity, both individually and corporately. Furthermore, these simple elements of creation are the symbols that we as Church use to weave and reweave relationships—with God and with each other—when we gather to celebrate the liturgy.

This paper explores three ideas: (1) the meaning of sacramentality and the importance of cultivating a sacramental worldview; (2) the centrality of the sacramental worldview within the Franciscan tradition; and (3) a way for Franciscans to approach worship, given our strong tradition of viewing life from a sacramental perspective.

---

[1] Many of the ideas in this article are more fully developed in Judith M. Kubicki, *The Presence of Christ in the Gathered Assembly* (New York: Continuum, 2006).

Sacramentality

I have the very good fortune of sometimes spending time at Cape Cod with a sister friend whose brother owns a house in Eastham. One of our vacation rituals is to get up before dawn and drive a few short miles to the beach to watch the sunrise. Oftentimes the fog or thick clouds prevent us from seeing the event for which we sacrificed precious sleep. Nevertheless, each morning we join the locals and tourists who come to the beach, often bracing in the wind, clutching their coffee cups and waiting in silence. Everyone's attention is fixed on the ocean's horizon in eager expectation of the first glimpse of the rising sun. When, on a clear day, it finally appears, a palpable experience of awe and wonder can be read in the faces and bodies of those who—especially in the summer months—have ventured out very early to witness this daily drama of promise and hope. Perhaps many of these "dawn seekers" rarely darken the threshold of a church. Yet, in this simple ritual of rising early and heading out to the water, they are drawn into an experience that opens them to an awareness of the sacred or the holy. Many might call this an experience of creation's innate sacramentality.

Let us begin, then, by reflecting on the notion of sacramentality. This first section will consider four aspects: the sacramentality of the universe, the need for contemplative openness, the importance of embodiment or bodiliness and the sacramentality of time. Having a sacramental worldview involves having our eyes and ears attuned to the intimations of a benevolent God who is always inviting us into a transforming relationship. Such a point of view requires an openness of the imagination to being constantly surprised by the presence of God in all the mundane elements of our existence. A sacramental perspective views the world as the locus where God reveals Godself and where we respond to that revelation.

The New Testament expresses the notion of sacramentality with the Greek word *mysterion*, meaning "hidden" or "secret." In his first letter to the Corinthians, Paul uses the word to speak about the hidden wisdom of God revealed through Christ's death and resurrection (1Cor. 2:7). Today we use the phrase "Paschal Mystery" in this same sense. The early Church used the Greek word *mysterion* within a worship context to speak about a variety of rites, symbols, liturgical objects, blessings and celebrations. But by the Middle Ages, the Latin translation for *mysterion*, that is, *sacramentum*, came to be restricted in its usage to refer only to official sacramental rites of the Church.[2]

In Kevin Irwin's judgment, the notion of sacramentality has diminished in the contemporary Christian imagination. Furthermore, he asserts that this notion must be retrieved if liturgy and sacraments are to survive as meaningful events in our contemporary world. This is critical because sacramentality is a particular way of seeing the world and looking at life. Indeed, it provides the framework not only for the way we live in the world and with each other but also for the way we celebrate our liturgical rites. A sacramental imagination is characterized by a profound awareness that the invisible divine presence is disclosed through visible created realities. Furthermore, a sacramental imagination takes seriously those everyday experiences that the Church appropriates to celebrate its life in God through the liturgy.[3] These experiences include bearing light, washing (or dunking), eating, drinking, and anointing with oil, among others. The ability to see these simple everyday actions as signs of the action of God in our lives presupposes a sacramental worldview. This is the basis for understanding our celebration of the liturgy as the mediation of the divine action within human rituals. We believe that the sacred is manifested in the secular; we perceive God as present and active in the world.

Our understanding of sacramentality, however, is not limited to an experience of God's presence in the world. No matter how much the sacred is mediated, either through ordinary human experience or through the symbolic activity of worship, no revelation of God can ever be complete or total. Therefore, alongside the experience of God's presence, there is also the experience of God's absence. Recall that the meaning of the Greek word *mysterion* is "hidden." The revelation of God's hiddenness is also an essential dimension of sacramentality. Even as sacramentality reveals that God is discoverable in the here and now, so too, sacramentality invites us to yearn for the fullness of God's presence, a fullness that can be attained only in eternity.[4] This awareness highlights the eschatological dimension of sacramentality.[5]

---

[2] Thomas P. Rausch, *Catholicism at the Dawn of the Third Millennium* (Collegeville, MN: Liturgical Press, 1996), 81.

[3] Kevin Irwin, "A Sacramental World—Sacramentality as the Primary Language of the Sacraments," *Worship* 76 (2002): 197-199. See also Rausch, 80.

[4] Irwin, 203.

[5] Eschatology is often understood as a theological study of the last things or the end times. However, its purview is much broader and richer than that. The word "es-

In other words, while the created world offers us glimpses of God's loving presence if we have the eyes to see, this experience is balanced by a longing for what can only be realized when we encounter God face to face. Nevertheless, the experience of God's absence is a positive rather than negative experience because it serves as a promise that what is glimpsed dimly in the present will be revealed when the need for sacraments shall cease.[6]

The Sacramentality of the Universe

The Franciscan Kenan B. Osborne builds his sacramental theology on a belief in the sacramentality of the universe. Indeed, Osborne views the sacramentality of the universe as the key to understanding the Church's sacraments in our contemporary world. He cautions, however, that we not forget that sacramentality is neither a thing, nor even a human action. Rather, sacramentality is "an action of God, a blessing, and a subsequent human response."[7] Furthermore, Osborne points out, God's action is always a "unique blessing/action that occurs at a unique time and in a unique space for unique people...." In other words, there is no "essential" general sacramentality. Rather both God's action and our response to God's action are "profoundly temporal, profoundly spatial, and profoundly relative."[8] This specificity of time and place, however, does not mean that we can think of God as occupying a localized position or site. Even when God communicates to human beings in a sacramental event, God is still experienced as hidden and ungraspable.[9] Nevertheless God's self-communication can only be experienced in the particularity of time, place and persons.

---

chatology" is derived from the Greek word "eschaton." This term highlights the fact that, since the paschal victory of Jesus Christ, we are living in the "end days." However, though Christ has already achieved this victory for us, it is not yet definitively accomplished. It is the difference or tension between the *already* and *not yet* that is designated by the term "eschatological."

[6] This sentiment is eloquently expressed in the last verse of William Turton's hymn text (1881), "Lord, Who in This Eucharist Didst Say." Some contemporary hymnals have dropped this verse, thereby losing this eschatological dimension.

[7] See Kenan B. Osborne, *Christian Sacraments in a Postmodern World: A Theology for the Third Millennium* (New York: Paulist Press, 1999), 50-53.

[8] Osborne, *Christian Sacraments*, 70-71.

[9] Lieven Boeve, "Thinking Sacramental Presence in a Postmodern Context: A Playground for Theological Renewal," in *Sacramental Presence in a Postmodern Context*, ed. L. Boeve and L. Leijssen (Leuven, Belgium: Leuven University Press, 2001), 21.

But even before Osborne, it was the twentieth-century theologian, Karl Rahner, who articulated the traditional Catholic belief in sacramentality within the larger context of "the infinitude of the world permeated by God."[10] For him, the fact that the world is permeated with grace makes it possible to believe in the grace of the sacraments. This is what Rahner means when he speaks of "the liturgy of the world."[11]

Today, however, in this postmodern period in which we live, theologians speak more tentatively about the world we live in as *possibly* a sacramental place. While the possibility exists that the world may be perceived this way, there is no guarantee that such an experience is either automatic or universal. Nevertheless, most of us would be inclined to acknowledge that there are moments in life when a person can experience sacramentality, and it is only because there are these moments that it is possible to speak meaningfully about a person, a church, or a ritual as sacramental.[12] This, in fact, is what post-Vatican II theologians and liturgists have been trying to promote: a viewpoint that perceives and celebrates the diffuse sacramentality of a life lived in faith.[13]

According to Louis-Marie Chauvet, a French sacramental theologian, whether or not the sacramentality of the world is perceived depends to a great extent on how human beings receive the world as creation, that is, as gift. According to Chauvet's schema, receiving the world as gift implies the necessity of return-gift. This sets up a dynamic that makes possible a vital relationship. Thus, for Chauvet, the doctrine of creation is itself charged with *sacramentality*, since it presupposes a relationship between God and humankind through the gift of creation. It is in the mystery of the liturgy that this mystery of creation finds its fullest expression when we pray through the words of the presider: "Blessed are you, Lord, God of all creation / through your goodness we have this bread to offer, / which earth has given and human hands have made." It is through such ritual action that faith confesses that God is creator.[14]

---

[10] Karl Rahner, "Considerations on the Active Role of the Person in the Sacramental Event," in *Theological Investigations,* Vol. 14, *Ecclesiology, Questions in the Church, the Church in the World,* trans. David Bourke (New York: Seabury Press, 1976), 169.

[11] Rahner, 166-169.

[12] Osborne, *Christian Sacraments,* 67.

[13] Louis-Marie Chauvet, *The Sacraments: The Word of God at the Mercy of the Body* (Collegeville, MN: Liturgical Press, 2001), xxii.

[14] Louis-Marie Chauvet, *Symbol and Sacrament: A Sacramental Reinterpretation of Christian Existence,* trans. Patrick Madigan and Madeleine E. Beaumont (Collegeville, MN: Liturgical Press, 1995), 551.

An appreciation for the sacramental structure of all creation is rooted in the perspective that all created reality is integral to the history of salvation. This view, which prevailed throughout the Patristic and Medieval periods (including the time of Francis and Clare, of course), locates the beginning of salvation with the creation of the world. Such thinking is rooted in New Testament creation theology, which is fundamentally a reflection on the meaning of Christ. Its purpose, according to Anne Clifford, "is to provide an interpretation of salvation in Jesus that is closely linked with creation, so closely linked that salvation is looked upon as a renewal of the original creation through the saving presence of God in Jesus."[15] For example, creation and redemption intersect in the phrase "new creation" when Paul exclaims: "So if anyone is in Christ, there is a new creation: everything old has passed away; see, everything has become new!" (2Cor. 5:17). Similarly, the notion of creation participating in the process of redemption is poetically expressed in the familiar passage from Romans:

> I consider that the sufferings of this present time are not worth comparing with the glory about to be revealed to us. For the creation waits with eager longing for the revealing of the children of God; for the creation was subjected to futility, not of its own will but by the will of the one who subjected it, in hope that the creation itself will be set free from its bondage to decay and will obtain the freedom of the glory of the children of God. We know that the whole creation has been groaning in labor pains until now; and not only the creation, but we ourselves, who have the first fruits of the Spirit, groan inwardly while we wait for adoption, the redemption of our bodies (Rom. 8:18-23).

Contemplative Openness

Another essential element for perceiving the sacramentality of life is the cultivation of a contemplative openness. Godfried Cardinal Danneels of Belgium acknowledges that maintaining a posture of contemplative openness is a serious challenge in the contemporary milieu. To highlight the fundamental quality of liturgical activity,

---

[15] Anne M. Clifford, "Creation," in *Systematic Theology: Roman Catholic Perspectives*, ed. Francis Schüssler Fiorenza and John P. Galvin, Vol. 1 (Minneapolis: Fortress Press, 1991), 209.

Danneels refers to those who participate in the liturgy, both individually and collectively, as *"homo liturgicus,"* that is, as human beings whose nature it is to "do liturgy." The fundamental attitude that Danneels identifies as required of *"homo liturgicus"* is receptivity, readiness to listen, self-giving and self-relativizing.[16] Danneels further describes this fundamental attitude as an

> orientation towards God, obedience, grateful reception, wonder, adoration, and praise. It is an attitude of listening and seeing, of what Guardini called "contemplating," an attitude so alien to the *"homo faber"* [human being as worker] in many of us.[17]

This openness or receptivity is intimately dependent on the experience of the senses, especially on listening and seeing.

Embodiment

Danneels's reflection on the importance of listening and seeing for promoting the contemplative attitude highlights the fact that it is the body—both individually and collectively—that is the location for the experience of sacramentality, that is, for an experience of the presence of God. Louis-Marie Chauvet highlights the importance of bodiliness when he explains that "the human being does not have a body, but is body."[18] Furthermore, this "I-body" or "person-as-body" exists only as woven, inhabited and spoken by the triple body of culture, tradition and nature. That is, human be-ing, as corporeal, is the place where the triple body—social, ancestral and cosmic—is symbolically joined.[19] Furthermore, Chauvet views the liturgy as that "powerful pedagogy where we learn to consent to the presence of the absence of God, who obliges us to give him a body in the world."[20]

Thus far we can say that the notion of sacramentality involves an appreciation of the significance of creation, particularly bodiliness, in communicating God's presence in the world. This aspect of bodiliness

---

[16] Godfried Cardinal Danneels, "Liturgy Forty Years after the Second Vatican Council: High Point or Recession," in *Liturgy in a Postmodern World*, ed. Keith Pecklers (New York: Continuum, 2003), 10.

[17] Danneels, 10.

[18] Chauvet, *Symbol and Sacrament*, 149.

[19] Chauvet, *Symbol and Sacrament*, 149-150.

[20] Chauvet, *Symbol and Sacrament*, 265.

or embodiment is, after all, the basis of the mystery of the Incarnation, of Christian faith in Jesus Christ as the Word made flesh. In this way, the privileged event of the Incarnation, as well as every other sacramental event, is an occasion of disclosure that can be interpersonal and revelatory because it assumes bodiliness. Furthermore, as Osborne reminds us, it cannot be an event in the abstract, but only in the concrete, since sacramentality always involves a particular or unique moment, place, person, or group of persons.[21]

The Sacramentality of Time

This reference to a "unique moment" raises an important point regarding time as sacramental. Recall the scene at Cape Cod described above. Without using the language, the beach dwellers who gather each morning for the sunrise (and there are others who gather on the bay side for sunset) acknowledge through their actions an intuitive sense of the sacramentality of creation and, more specifically, of the sacramentality of time. Since time is a part of creation and all creation has the potential to manifest the love, mercy and goodness of God, it seems that on some level, at least, we can speak of time as sacramental.

Traditionally, the Church has spoken of the fact that worship and, more specifically, the practice of daily prayer such as the Liturgy of the Hours, "sanctifies" or "consecrates" time. Our contemporary experience of time is usually one in which we are attempting to "beat the clock," "save time," or "defy aging." However, humankind's relationship with time has not always been so adversarial. Ancient civilizations were more in tune with the ways in which the cosmic dimensions of time directly related to human experience. There are, however, those rare moments when time is an epiphany of some deeper reality, and we sense that time stands still. In moments of deep human joy and suffering, poetry and drama, awe and wonder, our perception of time changes and we find ourselves capable of living life more fully.[22] Shortly before he died in battle, a young soldier wrote a letter in which he expressed a depth of awareness of the significance of time well beyond his years. This is an excerpt:

---

[21] See Osborne, *Christian Sacraments*, 70-71.

[22] George Guiver, *Company of Voices: Daily Prayer and the People of God* (New York: Pueblo Publishing Co., 1988), 14.

We make the division between life and death as if it were one of dates—being born at one date and dying some years after. But just as we sleep half our lives, so when we're awake, too, we know that often we're only half alive. Life, in fact, is a quality rather than a quantity, and there are certain moments of real life whose value seems so great that to measure them by the clock, and find them to have lasted so many hours or minutes, must appear trivial and meaningless. Their power, indeed, is such that we cannot properly tell how long they last, for they can colour all the rest of our lives, and remain a source of strength and joy that you know not to be exhausted, even though you cannot trace exactly how it works.[23]

Such depth of insight into the nature of time can be rare in our technological, efficiency-driven world. Nevertheless, the possibility of perceiving time as sacramental invites us to enter into a different relationship with time. In such a relationship, the passage of time and our experience of its rhythm or fixed intervals offer glimpses of God's action and presence in the ordinariness of our lives. When this happens, the *"chronos"* (measured time) of our daily existence intersects on some level with God's time or *"kairos."* In this way the regular temporal rhythms of gathering for Eucharist or the Liturgy of the Hours can themselves become a sacramental framework that mediates an encounter with the Risen Christ.

When we gather for worship, we are, in one sense, disengaging from measured time (*chronos*)—the type to which we can easily become enslaved—and entering into an experience of eternity manifested in the present moment (*kairos*). Our focus is God's Kingdom glimpsed in time.[24] Feasts and seasons situate the liturgical assembly through time-oriented texts that mediate the tension between the "already and not-yet" of God's gift of salvation embodied in the person of Jesus Christ. Therefore, even as we celebrate and acknowledge Christ's presence, his absence "until he comes again" is deeply felt. It is this longing for the fullness of Christ's presence already glimpsed "as through a glass darkly"[25] that provides the eschatological thrust

---

[23] Quoted in John Westerdale Bowker, *Problems of Suffering in Religions of the World* (Cambridge: Cambridge University Press, 1970), 91.

[24] John Melloh, "Liturgical Time, Theology of," in *The New Dictionary of Sacramental Worship*, ed. Peter E. Fink (Collegeville, MN: Liturgical Press, 1990), 733.

[25] See 1Cor. 13:12-13.

toward the final coming of the reign of God. This is what the sacramentality of time is all about.

The Franciscan Tradition as Expressed in the Theology of Bonaventure

While Francis lived a spirituality that was expressive of a sacramental worldview, it is Bonaventure who offers us the theological foundations for Francis's spirituality. There are certain elements in Bonaventure's theology that are key to identifying the sacramental aspects of his thinking. These include his strong Christocentric perspective, his creation theology and his emphasis on the role of the senses and the affections in the Christian life.

The Incarnation

Bonaventure's theological perspective is decidedly Christocentric. The figure of Christ is the center or point of convergence of all that makes up created reality. Further, this theological vision is cosmic in proportions since the Incarnation is understood as the ultimate perfection of creation.[26] By understanding the primary reason for the Incarnation in terms of cosmic completion, Bonaventure highlights the profound role of the human person in creation, since the human person alone is created congruent to the Word of God.[27] Contemporary theologians such as Karl Rahner and Edward Schillebeeckx have expressed this insight in yet another way when they speak of Jesus Christ as primordial sacrament. In other words, we can experience the world as the location of God's grace and the sacraments as meeting places between God and humankind, because Jesus Christ in his humanity is the revelation of God. In other words, all other sacraments have their meaning only through the sacramentality of Jesus.[28] Putting Christ at the center in this way corresponds with Bonaventure's description of Christ as center and point of convergence of all of created reality.

---

[26] Zachary Hayes, *The Gift of Being: A Theology of Creation*, New Theology Studies, gen. ed. Peter Phan, no. 10 (Collegeville, MN: Liturgical Press, 2001), 104.

[27] Ilia Delio, *Simply Bonaventure: An Introduction to His Life, Thought, and Writings* (Hyde Park: NY: New City Press, 2001), 14.

[28] Kenan B. Osborne, *Sacramental Theology: A General Introduction* (New York: Paulist Press, 1988), 76.

Creation

Even those who know very little about Franciscanism know that Francis of Assisi is associated with a love for creation. In many areas of the country each fall, various media feature human-interest stories that report churches sponsoring the annual blessing of animals. Each year in Manhattan, the two major Episcopal churches, The Cathedral of St. John the Divine and St. Bartholomew's, delight New York pet owners by holding a special blessing of animals in observance of the feast of Francis. Furthermore, sightings of St. Francis statues in backyards, gardens and birdbaths can be made in nearly any city and suburban neighborhood. The theological and spiritual richness underlying both these popular practices demands that we move beyond pious stereotypes. Bonaventure's articulation of Francis's theology of creation provides us with the solid foundation that one hopes inspires such practices of popular religion.

According to Ilia Delio, Bonaventure views creation as a *theophany*, that is, as an expression of God's glory manifested in the order of creation.[29] This expression is Christocentric since, for Bonaventure, the entire cosmos is an expression of the Word, that is, of Christ. In the same way that the Word expresses the Father, creation appears as the divine ideas of the Word. In this way, creation appears as the art of God.[30] Delio explains:

> This means that everything in creation has its model or exemplar in the Word of God. When the Word becomes flesh, the center of the Trinity in which the truth of all reality exists, appears at the center of creation; thus, the truth of creation is revealed.[31]

And so, since the Word of God is expressed in boundless ways in creation, Bonaventure views the world as sacramental. In other words, creation in all its ordinariness is, for him, symbolic and full of signs of God's presence. Bonaventure refers to these mundane or ordinary created realities as symbols or windows into the divine.[32]

---

[29] Delio, *Simply Bonaventure*, 61.
[30] Delio, *Simply Bonaventure*, 60.
[31] Delio, *Simply Bonaventure*, 60.
[32] See Zachary Hayes, *Mystical Writings*, The Spiritual Legacy Series (New York: Crossroad Publishing Co., 1999), 66-67. An excerpt from Bonaventure's *Collations on the Six Days of Creation* regarding creation as a window into the divine is offered in transla-

Recall that the thirteenth century witnessed the construction of glorious French gothic structures, particularly the cathedral of Notre Dame and the Sainte Chapelle. The windows of these buildings present the visitor with a magnificent display of richly colored light. Its varied hues and tones shift with the sun's movement (or, more accurately, the movement of the earth around the sun). It was in 1273 in Paris, where both of these churches are located, that Bonaventure delivered his reflections on creation, including a discussion on the metaphor of the window.[33] In addition, in still other places, Bonaventure expresses this relationship between God and creation by referring to the universe as a mirror, footprint, or book that reveals its Creator.[34]

The Soul's Journey into God

Lastly, Bonaventure identifies a strong affective dimension coupled with an appreciation for the role of our five senses as essential to developing a relationship with God. This is particularly evident in the *Itinerarium mentis in Deum* (*The Soul's Journey into God*), a work in which Bonaventure presents a theological vision that sees God reflected throughout the created universe—a typical Franciscan view.[35] Ewert Cousins summarizes the *Itinerarium's* inherent Franciscan understanding of sacramentality when he explains that the book

> expresses the Franciscan awareness of the presence of God in creation; the physical universe and the soul are seen as mirrors reflecting God and as rungs in a ladder leading to God. Bonaventure expresses here, in his own way, Francis's joy in the sacrality and sacramentality of creation and, in so doing, captures an essential element in Franciscan spirituality. Basic though this element is, it would not be complete without its flowering in devotion to the humanity of Christ. There is a natural link between the Franciscan attitude toward material creation, as sacramentally manifesting God, and the Francis-

---

tion here. See also Hayes, *A Window to the Divine: A Study of Christian Creation Theology* (Quincy, IL: Franciscan Press, 1997).

[33] Hayes, *Mystical Writings*, 66.

[34] See Delio, 61-62 and Hayes, *Window to the Divine*, xii.

[35] *Bonaventure: The Soul's Journey into God, the Tree of Life, The Life of St. Francis*, trans., Ewert Cousins (Mahwah, NJ: Paulist Press, 1978), xix.

can devotion to the incarnation as the fullness of this manifestation.[36]

For Bonaventure, as for Francis, a theology of creation is clearly linked with a theology of the Incarnation. And this link informs Bonaventure's understanding of sacramentality in the *Itinerarium*.

Franciscan Worship in the Contemporary Church

So what does this mean for Franciscan worship today? It means, I believe, that we as Franciscans need to approach the liturgy with a deeper awareness of our tradition and a willingness to live out its implications in the way we approach worship. And, if Kevin Irwin is correct—as I believe he is—we need to begin by nurturing a sacramental imagination. This is the foundation for authentic worship and, based on some of the aspects of our tradition as reviewed here, this should be second nature for Franciscans. As followers of Francis of Assisi, it is our vocation to live in a profound awareness of the many and varied ways in which the invisible divine presence is disclosed through visible created realities. It is our vocation to view the world as the location where God reveals Godself and where we respond to that revelation.

A sacramental worldview will enable us to celebrate liturgy more authentically because it will ground our worship in a fundamental reverence for the created world and in a deep appreciation for embodiment or bodiliness. These qualities are essential for worship since, when we gather to celebrate the liturgy, we are engaging in ritual behavior that involves the interplay of symbols. Furthermore, these symbols are rooted in creation and speak to a "human be-ing-ness" that is bodily.

The dynamism of this interplay of symbols can perhaps be more easily understood by comparing it with a fundamental principle of quantum physics:

> Quantum physics describes the universe as a place where everything is interconnected or interrelated. Connections are realized by energy concentrated in bundles called "quanta" that flow throughout all of reality. Indeed, this energy is the primary essence of reality. It is an astounding and fresh way

---

[36] *Bonaventure*, 13.

to look at the cosmos! The notion that all of reality is interdependent and that its relatedness is accomplished by means of the flow of energy provides an apt metaphor for understanding the symbolic activity that occurs in the liturgy. Like the bundles of energy described in quantum theory, liturgical symbols interact with each other, transferring and increasing energy, shedding light, and unfolding meaning.[37]

One of the results of engaging in the symbolizing activity that we call worship is building a sense of identity and a network of relationships, not only within and between individuals, but also between persons and God. In other words, the symbolic activity of the liturgy helps to build the Church. If this be the case, then the way we celebrate symbols is not just a matter of aesthetics or good order. Rather, it reaches to the heart of who we are as Church and, in our case, who we are as Franciscans. Furthermore, while signs (such as traffic signs or exit signs) function on the level of cognition, providing us with information, symbols function on the level of recognition, providing us not with information, but with integration. This integration occurs both on the personal and interpersonal level, that is, both within a person and between persons.[38]

Bodiliness is an important aspect of our celebration of these symbols. We are not talking about cerebral activity. Rather, symbols include the gestures, postures and actions that are (in the words of our U.S. bishops) the "physical, visible, and public expressions by which human beings understand and manifest their inner life."[39] This is necessarily the case because celebrating the liturgy is an exhibitive rather than assertive activity.

Chauvet reminds us that embodied expression (e.g., gestures and postures) is at the heart of communal symbolic activity. Furthermore, such activity can rightly be described as exhibitive. Worship is exhibitive because it involves symbolic activity. An activity is exhibitive

---

[37] Judith M. Kubicki, *The Presence of Christ in the Gathered Assembly* (New York: Continuum, 2006), 125. My applying the insights of quantum physics to theology is derived from the following: Diarmuid O'Murchu, *Quantum Theology: Spiritual Implications of the New Physics,* revised (New York: Crossroad, 2004), 29-30.

[38] See a more detailed discussion of Michael Polanyi's semiotics in Judith Marie Kubicki, *Liturgical Music as Ritual Symbol: A Case Study of Jacques Berthier's Taizé Music, Liturgia condenda* 9 (Leuven, Belgium: Peeters Publishers and Booksellers, 1999), 97-100.

[39] United States Conference of Catholic Bishops, *Built of Living Stones: Art, Architecture, and Worship* (Washington, DC: USCCB, 2000), art. 22.

when it does not explain what something means, but expresses it or exhibits it. So, for example, a man could (conceivably) read a treatise on love to the woman who is the object of his affection. Or, he could simply kiss the woman. The first behavior—reading the treatise—would be communicating in a discursive, assertive, or prepositional manner (more cerebral, if you will). The second option—the kiss—is exhibitive.

So it is by means of gestures and postures that faith is both expressed and shaped in an exhibitive way. While this may be non-discursive, it is yet articulate. What is at issue in celebrating the liturgy authentically is how standing, kneeling, processing, bowing, proclaiming, listening, eating, drinking, speaking and singing—and doing it together—promote awareness of Christ's presence within the community. We have come full circle. We are looking once again at the revelation of Christ's presence through a sacramental celebration of the simple elements of creation.

Another example may further illustrate the meaning of "exhibitive." We exhibit the meaning of Easter through fire, water, gesture, color, music, proclamation, storytelling, etc. The purpose of the Easter Vigil is not to tell the story of the Resurrection to people who don't already know it, but to allow those who believe it to express or manifest or exhibit that belief. So the Paschal Mystery is "danced out, sung out, sat out in silence, or lived out liturgically,"[40] with ideas playing a secondary role. This is what it means to truly celebrate the symbols of the liturgy. This is how we celebrate the presence of Christ in our midst.

Liturgical symbols include such elements of creation as water, fire, bread, wine and oil. They also include architecture, texture, color, sound, silence, music, the scent of incense, sacred vessels, the crucifix, altar, books, vestments, the presider and, above all, the assembly. There is a clear and tangible sense of embodiment about our worship if we only pay attention. This is where we engage our sacramental imagination. But there is an important qualification to be made. These symbols need to be celebrated with largesse, with a magnanimity that acknowledges that they are the mediators of a *"sacrum commercium,"* that is, a sacred exchange between God and humankind.

Niggardliness, artificiality, or reduction of symbols can only inhibit their ability to perform as sacraments of our encounter with the divine. This is a case where less is *not* more. Rather, use plenty

---

[40] See Tom Driver, *The Magic of Ritual: Our Need for Liberating Rites that Transform Our Lives and Our Communities* (San Francisco: HarperCollins, 1991), 84.

of water and oil for baptism, burn real candles, decorate with fresh flowers, process with grace and dignity, enter into communal prayer with generous amounts of silence, begin the Easter Vigil in the dark, build dramatic Easter fires, make music that erupts from the depths of our being, proclaim the Scriptures with care and conviction, preside at prayer with gracious gestures and postures, respect the hour of the day for the celebration of the Liturgy of the Hours. These are some of the ways that our sacramental imagination can be both fed and expressed. We can only know our Christian faith in and through our bodies.

So we need to take symbols seriously and celebrate them well. We need to do this because we have bodies. Symbols are the means by which we get in touch with the presence of God that, like the illusiveness of energy, permeates all of creation, but can only be apprehended when it is embodied.

CHAPTER THREE

FRANCISCAN THEOLOGY OF THE EUCHARIST: DOES IT INFORM OUR LIVES?

James G. Sabak, O.F.M.

Writing a paper that answers the question whether or not the Eucharist informs the lives of Franciscans faces two distinct hurdles. On the one hand, it is a loaded question that can be construed as license to make judgments based on the experiences of Eucharistic practices of various communities of Franciscans. Such an approach would probably not endear me to many Franciscan communities, since it is my experience that there are occasions when friars find the liturgy a more contentious topic to discuss than poverty. On the other hand, it is a daunting question, because this topic is a field little mined at present. In this regard, I am entering into new territory, albeit only in a modest way, and so feel some trepidation.

Yet, the question of the impact of a theology of the Eucharist on the Franciscan movement and its continued influence in our own day is a topic worthy of investigation and reflection. I write this at a point in history when questions of lost, forgotten and suppressed information within the greater Catholic religious tradition consume the attention of both the culture and the academy. It is, therefore, both providential and appropriate to ponder again what comprises a specifically "Franciscan" Eucharistic theology, how it impacted the early Franciscan movement and how it informs and challenges us today. This paper, then, will consist of three parts. Part One will provide a brief analysis of the medieval social and liturgical context in which Francis and the early Franciscan Movement understood, celebrated and engaged in the Eucharist. Part Two will offer a description of five aspects of Franciscan Eucharistic theology, gleaned from the analysis in Part One. Part Three will assess the role of the Eucharist in some contemporary Franciscan and ecclesial contexts.

Part One: The Medieval Context

Kevin W. Irwin in his book, *Context and Text*, writes that when speaking about matters sacramental and liturgical, it is important to consider the context, especially social and cultural, in which these theologies and practices evolved. Attention to such concerns reveals some of the ways the act of liturgy influences the shape of theology and how we live the moral, spiritual life.[1] It is well, then, to begin our consideration by examining how liturgy influenced the evolution of our Franciscan tradition and charism. While eight hundred years of history and tradition may be a bit intimidating to traverse, I will focus on the late twelfth and early thirteenth centuries, in which our tradition finds its origins. This historical period holds a key in retrieving and revealing what may have been overlooked in the development of a uniquely Franciscan engagement with the Eucharist. We are inheritors of a medieval understanding of creation and the cosmos, an understanding perhaps all too easily dismissed today as benighted or ignorant, yet one that greatly influenced and continues to influence how Franciscans enact the Eucharist.

In my province, particularly in our houses of formation, we have added, at morning and evening prayer, an intercession for vocations to all families of the Order. Every Thursday morning we pray this particular intercession:

> O God, Francis and Clare had great awe and reverence for the Eucharist: may our devotion to Jesus' Body and Blood be an example to those who aspire to the Franciscan life.

Captured in this intercession, I believe, lies the kernel of our investigation and the answer to our question. Yet its key words—*awe*, *reverence* and *devotion*—translate very differently today than they did in Francis's time. Today, one might primarily associate "awe," "reverence" and "devotion" with a privatized idea of the Eucharist and associate them with a celebration of solemn exposition of the Holy Eucharist. For St. Francis, however, these were emotions and evocations integral to the context of a communal experience of the Eucharist.

In order to appreciate this distinction, it is important to overcome two suppositions about the medieval period that often complicate a

---

[1] Kevin W. Irwin, *Context and Text: Method in Liturgical Theology* (Collegeville: The Liturgical Press, 1994), 55.

full appreciation of a Franciscan appropriation of the Eucharist. The first is the belief that during this period a sharp division occurred between clergy and laity, resulting in the latter becoming a passive, non-participative body, largely ignored by the clerical classes who conducted the liturgy. It is believed that this situation led the lay faithful to adopt quasi-magical and superstitious devotional practices that further weakened the communal structure of Eucharistic celebration. The second supposition is that Francis needed intense and frequent times of contemplative solitude throughout his life. This seems more consistent with a privatized rather than communal engagement with the Eucharist and the liturgy.

In addressing the first supposition, it is important to stress that the High Middle Ages encapsulated a tremendous period of social transformation, religious challenge, doctrinal development and creativity in spirituality. While it was a time of consternation, fear and unrest, it was also a time of revolution in the realm of piety and devotion. It initiated the reform of many abuses in religious practices.[2] This period witnessed the rise of new religious movements as well as new social classes and societal relationships. For the purposes of this paper, I note that the religious and spiritual milieu also was subject to new directions. Josef Jungmann describes the religious context clearly:

> A consequence of the exertion of papal prerogatives over royal and princely control in the 11th and 12th centuries allowed a temporal, organizational aspect of Church to stand in the foreground. The stress on this temporal character and an accompanying juridical-hierarchical apparatus lead to the coming into prominence of the contrast between clergy and laity. ... In some measure, the idea of a holy people who are close to God as the priest is, has become lost. The Church begins to be chiefly represented by the clergy.... The Spiritual nature of the Church was partly clouded over.[3]

A strong emphasis on distinguishing between clergy and laity brought with it a corresponding sense that some individuals were holier than others and, therefore, more worthy to receive spiritual ben-

---

[2] See Giles Constable, *The Reformation of the Twelfth Century* (Cambridge: Cambridge University Press, 1996), 88-124; and R. N. Swanson, *Religion and Devotion in Europe c. 1215-1515* (Cambridge: Cambridge University Press, 1995), 15-41.

[3] Josef A. Jungmann, *Pastoral Liturgy* (New York: Herder and Herder, 1962), 59, 60, 62.

efits than others. Preoccupation with the impact of such perceptions spilled over into liturgical practice and dogmatic understanding of the sacraments, especially in regard to the manner of sharing in and comprehending the Eucharist, a privileged sacrament.

Eventually this preoccupation led to a paradoxical development. Various controversies surrounding the presence of Christ in the Eucharist gave rise to an expansion of a highly specified understanding of this presence,[4] which was doctrinally affirmed by the Fourth Lateran Council in 1215. Such a strong emphasis on the presence of Christ in the Eucharist translated into highly specified norms for worthy reception of the sacrament.[5] As this enhanced significance of the Eucharistic presence developed, so too did the notion that Eucharistic liturgical rituals were the preserve of the clergy, who protected them and officiated at them. Consequently, many of its aspects were withdrawn from lay participation.[6] Fear of receiving the sacrament unworthily and suffering repercussions for so doing lessened frequent reception of communion among the faithful. Eventually, they had to be urged to receive communion at least once a year.[7]

As deconstructive as these developments in Eucharistic practice seem today, it may be too simplistic to say that they were the machinations of power hungry and insensitive clerics seeking to make unwitting dupes of the faithful. In point of fact, the clergy believed that they were doing what was best for the spiritual welfare of the faithful. As Chrysogonus Waddell says:

> The 12th century distinction between cleric and layman was not meant (in theory) to deny the layman participation in the

---

[4] One of the most celebrated was the controversy initiated by Berengarius of Tours (11th century), who taught a symbolic presence of Christ in the Eucharist that concentrated more on the change of participants in the Eucharistic liturgy than on the species of bread and wine. His teaching was felt to threaten the Church's teaching on the real presence of Christ at the time and was condemned.

[5] See Thomas Aquinas, *De eucharista ad modum decem praedicamentorum, sive De corpore Christi*; Nicolaus de Lyra, *Dicta de sacramento. – Expositio orationis dominicae* (Imprint: Cologne: Heinrich Quentell, 1490). Among such requisites are mental competence, fasting devoutly, freedom from any awareness of mortal sin, freedom from guilt of notorious crimes, and having a clean body.

[6] Miri Rubin, *Corpus Christi: The Eucharist in Late Medieval Culture* (Cambridge: Cambridge University Press, 1991), 70. One of these consequences was that throughout the 12th century the chalice was removed from communion of the laity and replaced with the theory of concomitance (i.e., the full presence of Christ is experienced in both the bread and the wine, so only one species was necessary).

[7] Jungmann, *Pastoral Liturgy*, 62.

liturgy, but to ensure his participation in the manner best suited to his lay estate.[8]

But, in spite of these unfolding circumstances, a longing for Holy Communion remained in the life of the great majority of non-ordained faithful and expressed itself in a fundamental desire and need to connect with the Eucharist and to celebrate it in a communal fashion.

Eventually, a wide range and variety of devotional practices and substitutes for sharing in the Eucharistic meal began to fill the unfortunate vacuum created by the separation of the faithful from direct participation in the Eucharistic celebration. Among these was an emphasis on the elevation of the Eucharistic elements—the bread and the wine—at the consecration.[9] This action engendered great devotion among the faithful, who substituted one sense for another in Eucharistic engagement. Gazing upon the elevated species took the place of physical reception of the sacrament. Such gazing was considered "participating" in the Eucharist. Some theologians and spiritual directors of the age even attached certain sacramental benefits to looking upon the Eucharist at Mass.[10] The faithful were encouraged to do so by the ringing of bells, the burning of incense and the lighting of candles during the elevation.[11] Such practice also led to the idea of "spiritual communion," in which the sacramental benefits of participation could be experienced even when one was not present at a Eucharistic liturgy or even in a church. This idea, however, was not predominant.

Visible or *ocular* communion, then, replaced physical communion as a type of reception in and of itself in order to keep the Eucharist as a public symbol and act of the Church. Francis, himself, would adopt this development to maintain the centrality of the Eucharist in all the

---

[8] Chrysogonus Waddell, "Reform of the Liturgy from a Renaissance Perspective," in *Renaissance and Renewal in the Twelfth Century*, ed. Robert L. Benson and Giles Constable (Toronto: University of Toronto Press, 1982; reprint 1999), 97.

[9] Rubin, *Corpus Christi*, 55. Although the origin of this liturgical action remains unclear, whether from the people's desire to "see God" or as a "didactic gesture against heretical claims," the gesture was incorporated into the liturgy in Paris by the early 1200s.

[10] The Franciscan theologians, Alexander of Hales and Bonaventure, rejected such assumptions. See Rubin, *Corpus Christi*, 64.

[11] Rubin, *Corpus Christi*, 58-61. It is interesting to note that prayers written for the laity to be prayed during the elevation are very focused on eating, tasting, feeding upon and consuming the Eucharistic elements. See David N. Power, *The Eucharistic Mystery: Revitalizing the Tradition* (New York: Crossroad Publishing Company, 1995), 188-189.

practices of the Order.[12] However, in the establishment of the greatest of all medieval Eucharistic celebrations, the Feast of Corpus Christi, there was resistance to understanding the feast as a visual replacement for reception of communion. Pope Urban IV, who instituted the feast, insisted on participation in the liturgy as the *ordinary norm* of Eucharistic piety and devotion. Processions, exposition and benediction with the Eucharist were regarded as *extraordinary* solemn actions.[13] The primary focus remained more on personal and participatory engagement with Christ present in a liturgical act than in receiving a spiritualized or imaginary aspect of sacramental communion. There was still an ardent and fervent desire for eternal union with Christ, the Word made Flesh, through communion.[14]

The patterns and practices of the thirteenth century reveal a Church caught between culture and mission. The ethos and temptations of the former ran toward amassing power, exercising control and writing legislation. The mission of evangelization, however, was founded in the strong communal, spiritual and participatory nature of Christ and the Holy Spirit. The resulting tension was experienced in all facets of the Church's life, but where it had the most impact was in the manner in which the Church celebrated the sacraments, particularly the Eucharist. What is amazing is that, in the midst of such tension and often excluded from receiving the sacrament of the Eucharist, the faithful did not abandon it. Rather, they contemplated and devoutly adored, even from a distance, and nurtured an intense, active and, in many respects, a very communal piety. This piety, while it would eventually lead to an overt cult of the Eucharist, could never have been construed as a privatization of Christian life and worship.[15]

Establishing the liturgical context of the medieval period of Franciscan origins allows us to address the second supposition encountered when speaking about Franciscan Eucharistic engagement—that of Francis's need for solitary contemplation. The sources all agree that, following his conversion, Francis spent an extraordinary amount of his life in personal and private prayer. William Short writes that while not all the sources agree on the specific amount of time spent in prayer, several refer to a series of "Lents" or forty-day periods throughout the year (five in all), during which Francis may have been given over

---

[12] Power, *The Eucharistic Mystery*, 201.

[13] Nathan Mitchell, *Cult and Controversy: The Worship of the Eucharist Outside Mass* (Collegeville: The Liturgical Press, 1990), 185.

[14] Power, *The Eucharistic Mystery*, 187-189.

[15] Jungmann, *Pastoral Liturgy*, 63.

to intense, personal and individual development of his relationship with God (more than half the year!).[16] This might lead some to surmise that participation in the Eucharist and the liturgy did not play an important role in the life of Francis. It might seem that he preferred life alone, cultivating a more privatized devotional life with God. Such an understanding fails to appreciate the intensely social and cultural communal context in which Francis lived. Francis never had any idea of being alone. Those who attempted to separate themselves from the Christian community, whether through dissent (such as the Cathars) or desire to reform practices and leadership (such as the Humiliati) would be those most suspected of heresy.

The intensely communal ethic of the medieval period is often lost on our modern minds. While divisions and distinctions among classes of peoples did exist, it was still a highly social age, enhanced by feasting and ritual, which defined both its social and spiritual parameters. Liturgical feasts and rituals outside the Eucharist reflected the communal dimension of the late medieval period (albeit in ways that also expressed its inconsistencies). They also preserved the participatory nature of worship (albeit in an imperfect manner at times), which was in danger of drying up altogether under misguided and ill-informed ecclesiastical leadership and doctrinal practice. As Robert Swanson writes:

> The mass did not just bring Christ down to earth. The celebration was more than an occasion or object of personal devotion; it was also a focus for a community in communion, even though priestly control over reception and rivalry over precedence in reception also imposed strains on that community. The effectiveness of the mass meant that it was needed often.... Its vital importance to society as a whole and for its individual members, made it the preeminent feature of medieval religion.[17]

While a multitude of factors, then, negatively influenced the efficaciousness of the Eucharistic liturgy and hampered its appropriation, the laity reacted by establishing alternative forms of benefiting from the Mass and from the sacrament. These forms were never meant to become privatized devotions, such as recitation of the rosary during

---

[16] William J. Short, *The Franciscans* (Collegeville: The Liturgical Press, 1989), 122.
[17] Swanson, *Religion and Devotion in Europe*, 138-9.

the liturgy has often become today. They were prayer forms and rituals centered on a corporate understanding of worship. Devotional prayer was understood to be an act of mediation on behalf of a community.[18] People of the High Middle Ages were conscious of the role they played in worship. Even if some strands of theology taught that the strength of the prayer of priests was more efficacious, this perspective was never considered to exclude the effectiveness of anyone else's prayers.[19] In fact, there were still many devout laymen and women at that time who never forgot that the Eucharist was *the* great sign of union with the risen Lord and with the Christian community.[20]

This short survey of the High Middle Ages demonstrates that an understanding and appreciation of the sacrament as the source, foundation and experience of unity remained within the body of believers even as a strong doctrinal emphasis on the physical presence of Christ in the Eucharist gave rise to the practice of infrequent reception of the sacrament. Christians continued to manifest vibrant devotional spirituality and communal displays of worship.[21] While the way they engaged in ritual may not have been the most advantageous means of manifesting the corporate nature of the sacrament, it was probably the only means available, particularly at a time of social and spiritual change.[22] In addition, the Eucharist, in its doctrines and devotion, also functioned as a litmus test of identity and belonging. Acceptance or non-acceptance of doctrines concerning belief in the physical presence of Christ in the sacrament became the mark of membership in the community. Anyone who challenged the claims surrounding Eucharistic presence was deemed at least suspect and at worst an enemy.[23]

Therefore, it seems clear that the Eucharist did, indeed, inform the early Franciscan movement. Such an affirmation, however, is based on the character and context of the time. It is true that the High Middle Ages witnessed hardening divisions between clergy, monks and lay faithful, which disconnected the fullness of liturgical life from lived Christian experience. Yet, we must not reduce the character of the time

---

[18] Theodor Klauser, *A Short History of the Western Liturgy: An Account and Some Reflections*, 2nd ed. (Oxford: Oxford University Press, 1979), 136.

[19] Power, *The Eucharistic Mystery*, 170, 171, 186-7.

[20] Gary Macy, *The Banquet's Wisdom: A Short History of the Theologies of the Lord's Supper* (Mahwah, New Jersey: Paulist Press, 1992), 129.

[21] Jean Cottiaux, "L'office Liégeois de la Fête-Dieu, sa valeur et son destin," *Revue d'histoire ecclésiastique*, 58 (1963): 26.

[22] Power, *The Eucharistic Mystery*, 202.

[23] Miri Rubin, "Corpus Christi: Inventing a Feast," *History Today*, 40 (July 1990): 16.

to images of muted passivity on the part of the faithful. We recognize how, like other groups in the twelfth and thirteenth centuries, Francis and the nascent Franciscan movement embraced alternative outlets that sought to express the centrality of the Eucharist in Christian life. But, unlike dissident alternatives, Francis adopted approaches to the Eucharist that did not separate him or the movement from the larger Church. Herein lies an important distinction, which I will address below.

Part Two: Aspects of Franciscan Eucharistic Theology

In light of the above, I have assembled five aspects of Franciscan Eucharistic Theology. These are not the sum total of the dimensions one might uncover from this investigation, but they stand out as significant in the development of the Franciscan charism and tradition. They are: 1) presence and union; 2) the great condescension of God; 3) the role of the symbolic; 4) the nature of the Eucharist as *gift*; and 5) the importance of order and communion.

Presence and Union

Western medieval men and women were preoccupied with the presence of Christ in the Eucharist. Yet for them this preoccupation never featured a static or isolated presence. Rather, medieval imagination understood that Christ's presence in the Eucharist was to, for and with another. For Franciscans, the foundation of this understanding was scriptural: "Behold, I am with you always, until the end of the age" (Mt. 28: 20).[24] This presence, which permeates history and time, continually *affects* and *effects* the missionary activity of the Church, which seeks to bring all creation into deeper, more profound union in Christ.

This "Christic" presence is also crucially linked to the humility of Christ, most evident in the sweep of the paschal mystery. From Incarnation to Cross to Eucharist, Christ again and again reveals the depth of his presence, but always as *Emmanuel*, a "presence-with-us." Franciscan discernment perceives and reverences this presence in all of the created order. As Ilia Delio describes it, Francis of Assisi set about calling his contemporaries to recognize the footprints of God in creation. Everything in creation spoke to Francis and in speaking led

---

[24] All scripture references are from the *New American Bible*.

him to contemplate God in the things of creation. Such contemplation permitted Francis a penetrating gaze that revealed to him the truth of reality. He realized that this revelation could be attained and integrated into one's life by following the footprints of Jesus Christ.[25]

The sacraments were the most profound of the footprints of Christ, because they were intense experiences of the dynamism of God in the created order. And the Eucharist itself was the principal localization of this presence because of the incarnational nature of revelation. For Francis, the Incarnation revealed the vibrant relational nature of a God who wished to share all that God is with creation. The Eucharist, because it conveyed the reality of Christ's presence to believers, became the locus for the incarnational relationship of God with creation. The God who, at each Eucharistic celebration becomes present in a unique part of our created world, with unique individuals, in a unique sacramental moment—this is the same God who created all things.[26] In this way, the Eucharistic presence is a presence that both initiates and maintains union through communion.

St. Bonaventure further intensifies the nature of presence in the Eucharist by emphasizing the aspects of food and tradition. For him, the Eucharist is a sign and sacrament of love that unites its recipients in ardent communion with Christ and with one another. It is through the Eucharist that Christ fulfills his promise made at the conclusion of Matthew's Gospel. He remains always with the Church both as an act of memory and as food to sustain and refresh the life of wayfarers.[27]

Yet for Bonaventure this presence is not static. Bonaventure conceived the Eucharist as an affective remembrance, a union of ardent love, both corporeal and tangible, and which dovetailed well with the practices and attitudes of popular devotion of the age. This was a period of intense transformation, characterized by the uncertainties of instability, social readjustment and cultural transition. Chronic frustration and anxiety played upon people's need for comfort and identity.[28] They sought relief from a potentially alienating situation by engaging and focusing their anxieties and energies upon the highest of religious activities, the Eucharist. Franciscans contributed to alleviating some of this anxiety by emphasizing the "doing" of Eucharist. Franciscans saw the Eucharist as an active remembering of a pres-

---

[25] Ilia Delio, *A Franciscan View of Creation: Learning to Live in a Sacramental World* (St. Bonaventure, NY: The Franciscan Institute, 2003), 16.

[26] Short, *The Franciscans*, 107.

[27] Power, *The Eucharistic Mystery*, 239.

[28] Mitchell, *Cult and Controversy*, 173.

ence that promised to remain always. They engaged in that communion (common union) in such a way that it became a truth and reality through remembering.

The Great Condescension of God

In contemporary contexts, the word "condescension" does not carry very positive connotations. In any thesaurus one finds as its synonyms: disdain, arrogance, superciliousness or aloofness. And yet, when expressed of God, this word connotes self-emptying, giving-over, giving away. Such an understanding was not lost upon medieval society and, in fact, was celebrated by them. The Incarnation demonstrated the depth and profundity of God's giving over of God's very self—an act that deeply impacted the consciousness of medieval men and women. Francis connected such condescension with Christ present in the Eucharist. In fact, the condescension of God in the Eucharist became the manner in which the promised presence of Christ could be continually maintained and engaged. Condescension, again, reinforced the idea of an active, not a static presence of Christ in the Eucharist. As Francis encouraged his followers in the first *Admonition*:

> Each day [the Son of God] Himself comes to us, appearing humbly; each day He comes down from the bosom of the Father upon the altar in hands of a priest. As He revealed Himself to the holy apostles in true flesh, so He reveals Himself to us now in sacred bread.... And in this way the Lord is always with His faithful, as He Himself said: Behold I am with you until the end of the age (Adm 1: 16-22).[29]

Here the Eucharist informed the Franciscan Movement with the great humility of a God who ceaselessly departs from the lofty realms of heaven to share the substance of his being with a creation that he both loves and nurtures. God's condescension assures that the Eucharist is an active presence. Francis points out that God continually comes to us, is continually made present to us, is continually engaging with and engaged by the faithful.

---

[29] All quotations from Francis's writings are from *Francis of Assisi: Early Documents*, ed. Regis Armstrong, Wayne Hellmann and William Short, vol. I (New York: New City Press, 1999).

The Role of the Symbolic

Valuing the symbolic dimensions of human life grounded the Franciscans' attitude toward the presence of Christ encountered in the Eucharist. Franciscan Eucharistic theology never embraced nor rested upon crass realism. Although in the twelfth and thirteenth centuries the power of symbol had weakened significantly from the role it played in antiquity, there remained a sense of the symbolic as that which directed one to the most true and the most real. Francis's conception of the footprints of God in creation was consistent with the symbolic imagination that allowed one to approach and then to apprehend the deeper meanings of creation.

The Franciscan attitude toward symbol put special emphasis on the one who *receives* the symbol. An authentic reception of the Eucharist was expressly dependent on the intention of the receiver. Franciscan theologians taught that there were, in fact, *degrees* of reception based upon one's engagement and recognition of the Eucharist.[30] Alexander of Hales held that if the recipient of the Eucharist recognized the sign values of the symbol, particularly through belief and love, then he or she would be able to intuit the full grace offered by a sacrament.[31] The Franciscan exegete, Nicholas of Lyra, Master at the University of Paris in 1309, furthered this understanding and described a number of conditions necessary for the fullest reception of the grace inherent in a sacramental encounter.[32] The greatest of these was that one be a human being and a believer. An individual sincerely embracing both dimensions would be able to move from the real to the symbolic and thereby open up new horizons for understanding.

What such an engagement allowed was an opportunity to live more deeply in the realm of the subjunctive, in the realm of the "what if?" This is a unique stance that moves us beyond the all too common realm of the indicative, the "what is," and awakens in us attitudes towards and perceptions of reality, truth, beauty and love that lie hidden in the fabric of creation.[33] Such a symbolic awakening lies at the heart of *dispositive grace* as it is understood by Bonaventure, Scotus and

---

[30] Gary Macy, *Treasures from the Storeroom: Medieval Religion and the Eucharist* (Collegeville: The Liturgical Press, 1999), 176.

[31] Macy, *Treasures from the Storeroom*, 176-177.

[32] See Nicholas of Lyra, *Dicta de Sacramento*, in note 5 above.

[33] For an excellent introduction to the engagement of the subjunctive in ritual, see Clifford Geetz, *The Interpretation of Cultures* (New York: Basic Books, Inc. Publishers, 1973), especially chapter four: "Religion as a Cultural System."

Alexander of Hales. This designation describes the work of the sacraments *disposing* recipients to become more ready to receive *grace*—the acknowledgement that one is deeply, passionately, exceedingly loved by God—and thereby enabled to act in and through that grace.[34] Such a disposition engages and enacts again and again the distinctly Franciscan ideal of sacrament and sacramental rite as *covenantal* encounter. This counters the principle of *instrumental causality*, which focuses too mechanically on *how something takes place* in sacramental symbol. Dispositive grace shifts the emphasis to *what happens when* the symbolic is employed: one begins to recognize and act upon the revelation of God's work in creation.

As medieval scholars began to focus more upon the instrumental nature of sacraments to the detriment of a covenantal sense of sacramental symbol, the Church experienced an unfortunate separation and distinction between sacraments as signs and sacraments as causes. This loss further weakened a "here and now" context for Eucharistic celebration and precipitated a stronger focus on the Eucharist as principally food for the life of heaven. Yet for medieval Franciscans the symbolic never rested solely with the elements in themselves. As symbols, Eucharistic bread and wine pointed to a reality beyond themselves and made possible a fuller sense of the communion that took place beyond the sacramental reception of the elements. Franciscans and other medieval peoples would have called this fuller understanding "spiritual communion." "Spiritual," in this sense however, cannot be thought of as a sentimental or a private involvement in the Eucharist, but rather a life of faith and charity. This type of communion strengthened and celebrated an active Christian life.[35] Symbolic engagement in Eucharist, then, gave impetus to the Franciscan mission to the poor and marginalized. It may also have influenced the great theological masters of the age. In this way, the Eucharist informed the early Franciscan movement through a deeper appreciation of and engagement in the symbolic dimension of all reality.

The Nature of Eucharist as Gift

The most profound of all the symbolic dimensions of the Eucharist, however, is the notion of "gift." For Francis, God was and is the

---

[34] Kenan Osborne, *Sacramental Theology: A General Introduction* (New York: Paulist Press, 1988), 55.

[35] Macy, *Treasures from the Storeroom*, 179.

"great-gifter." God bows down in compassion and love to offer God's innermost reality as gift: in the Incarnation, in the Passion, in the Resurrection. This offering of self is the totality of the Paschal Mystery, revealed and made significant in the lives of believers.[36] Understanding gift-giving made the lifelong process of conversion possible, a conscious movement away from sin-centered attitudes and behaviors toward God-centered relationships.[37] In the Eucharist this "gift-ing" is continued. In the Eucharist a full giving over of Christ in bread and wine acts to nourish and sustain believers in and through a share in divine life for all creatures.[38] This, in turn, allows all creatures to discern and reverence the presence of God in one another.

It is John Duns Scotus who develops the profound idea of gift within the particular context of *haecceitas* ("thisness")—the acknowledgement that each human person is endowed with a unique value and dignity as one singularly wanted by and loved by God, quite apart from any trait one shares or contribution one makes.[39] The Eucharist encapsulates the nature of God's condescension, of God's giving-over of self as gift, as an act of God's absolute freedom, which in turn brings to realization that everything in creation is grace, unmerited gift.

Coupled with this is Scotus's understanding of *contingency*—everything depends on God. Nothing in the world is necessary, but all depends upon the compassion, mercy and love of God who brought it all into being. The concepts of gift and contingency applied to the Eucharist help the recipient recognize the profound and humbling dimensions of God's affection and desire for union with him or her. Sharing in the Eucharist, one is relieved of vain and purposeless striving. It allows one to return to God, in whom one finds the true depth of necessity and the true depth of freedom.[40] Francis recognized that such was the situation in all reality. Thus his references were always away from himself and towards God. He described his experiences as "The Lord gave me.... "

---

[36] Short, *The Franciscans*, 106.

[37] Delio, *A Franciscan View of Creation*, 11. See also Louis-Marie Chauvet, *The Sacraments: The Word of God at the Mercy of the Body* (Collegeville: The Liturgical Press, 2001), especially chapter six, "Symbolic Exchange."

[38] Short, *The Franciscans*, 107.

[39] Allen B. Wolter, *Duns Scotus' Early Oxford Lecture on Individuation* (Santa Barbara, CA: Old Mission Santa Barbara, 1992), xxvii. Kenan B. Osborne refers to this work in his study, *The Franciscan Intellectual Tradition: Tracing Its Origins and Identifying Its Central Components* (St. Bonaventure, NY: The Franciscan Institute, 2003), 67.

[40] Osborne, *The Franciscan Intellectual Tradition*, 68.

In this way, the Eucharist informed the early Franciscan Movement with a profound sense of freedom and humility.

The Importance of Order and Communion

In a contemporary ecclesiological context, it may also be difficult for us to relate the concept of "order" to the concept of communion. They are seen as exclusive. Yet for the medieval mentality, order and communion were mutually integrative and attuned. They found their origin in the understanding of gift and contingency. The divine "ordering" of the universe held a primary place in the medieval concept of self and creation, the maintenance of which was an overriding concern for all members of society. In a well-ordered Aristotelian universe, there was a place for everything and everything had a place.[41] This worldview, far from limiting participation in society, enabled one to contribute to the good of the community by fulfilling one's role according to one's place in the cosmic order.[42] Hence, there existed an urgent need to maintain "correct operation and attention" to one's responsibility within one's order. What might appear to the contemporary mind as a system of sectarianism was actually reflective of the social norms of the age.[43] As a result, medieval society oriented its cultural rituals and feasts toward the structured support of this order, with the Eucharist as its center. All participants in this system had a sense of belonging and, contrary to some assessments, experienced a solid interconnectedness, albeit based upon distinctions in hierarchical relationships.[44]

As a result of its appreciation of the Eucharist, the Franciscan Movement contributed a very significant element to the dynamic of this ordered society. On the one hand, Francis upheld the dimensions of order that made for the continued welfare of society, especially in the structures of the Church. Wishing to differentiate and distance himself from dissident groups that sought to undermine ecclesial structures and leadership, Francis remained ever affirming of his and the Order's place within the greater Church. This affirmation is often expressed in Francis's writings, where he especially asks his brothers

---

[41] Otto von Simson, *The Gothic Cathedral: Origins of Gothic Architecture and the Medieval Concept of Order* (Princeton: Princeton University Press, 1988), 28-29.

[42] Malcom Barber, *The Two Cities: Medieval Europe 1050-1320* (London: Routledge, 1992), 24-25.

[43] Power, *The Eucharistic Mystery*, 205.

[44] See chapter eight in Power, *The Eucharistic Mystery*, 163-183: "The Role of the Eucharist in Church and Society."

to respect and obey the clergy (*Second Letter to the Faithful*, *Earlier Rule 19*, *Letter to the Entire Order*, *Testament* and *Admonition* 26).

On the other hand, Francis and the early Franciscans were keenly aware of divisions occurring within the Church, particularly with regard to the Eucharist. In this regard, Francis brought a new kind of life to the sacrament through devotion to the reserved species; and in his own way bypassed clericalization. Reservation of the sacrament gave laypersons a certain freedom in their Eucharistic devotion, a relative independence from clergy and direct access to the Eucharist at any time or place. Francis "tweaked" the liturgical practices of his time. He applied the communal dimensions characteristic of eucharistic worship to engagements with the reserved species.[45]

In this regard, Franciscan eucharistic devotion embraced *communio* and never a privatized *"co-unio."* As David Power remarks: "The Eucharist was placed at the heart of Franciscan evangelical aspirations without indulging in criticism of the clergy or dissent from their authority, thereby maintaining and remaining in communion with the Church and its pastors."[46] In this way, the Eucharist informed the early Franciscan Movement by insisting that access to a sacrament whose purpose and goal was the creation of communion could not be procured by breaking that communion.

Summary

These five aspects played a formative role in the development of a Franciscan Eucharistic theology in the twelfth and thirteenth centuries. Yet after the fourteenth century, these insights were gradually lost or forgotten. Following the religious tumults of the sixteenth century, the Eucharist became regarded more as spectacle than as sacred action.[47] The *actio* (act) of Eucharist as the heart and soul of what a community is as the Body of Christ was transformed into *regula* (rule), or worse, *obligatio*—(obligation). The necessity of celebrating Eucharist now arises less from the need to reveal and discern the footprints of God in creation and more from an obligation one is under pains to fulfill. The ascendancy of Thomism as the interpretive key for understanding sacramental action and a diminishment in the influence of Franciscan theological masters contributed to obscuring the singular-

---

[45] Power, *The Eucharistic Mystery*, 200.
[46] Power, *The Eucharistic Mystery*, 200.
[47] See James F. White, *Roman Catholic Worship: Trent to Today,* 2nd ed. (Collegeville: The Liturgical Press, 2003), 2-5.

ity of Franciscan reflection on the Eucharist. As changing models influenced the Franciscan tradition more, the Eucharist informed Franciscan life less. It became something to which Franciscan ritual must *conform* in practice and rubric.

Part Three: Contemporary Eucharistic Engagement

Today, a Franciscan approach to Eucharistic engagement still labors under a variety of interpretations. In the forty plus years since the close of the Second Vatican Council, liturgy has played a vibrant and energizing role in many Franciscan communities. Still I wonder if this stems more from a desire to adopt the reforms than to reclaim the dynamic aspects of our tradition. I believe there remains an unfortunate ignorance concerning the contributions of the Franciscan theological tradition to liturgy, which may result in misinterpreting the conciliar liturgical reforms.

For example, there may be an impression that Franciscan liturgy is "simple" liturgy, where less is more, and that unelaborated or unadorned prayer is the best way to express poverty. This may not be so much an expression of Franciscan poverty as an impoverishment of liturgy. Liturgical rites are neither simple nor extravagant; they simply are. A remark such as, "I like *simple* liturgy better than *big* liturgy," might just translate into a Mass or liturgy that is private, quiet, reserved, contemplative. However, such a notion of "simple" could not fully describe the evolution of the Franciscan liturgical tradition, nor could it do justice to Francis's attitudes toward the Eucharist and liturgy. For him, as for *Lumen gentium* (1964), the full experience of liturgy is engaged through the gathering of the Communion, the Body of Christ: pope, bishops, presbyters, deacons, lectors, acolytes, ministers of Holy Communion *and* the faithful—all enacting their own roles with sincerity and authenticity! (See *Lumen gentium*, Chapter 3.)

A Franciscan theology of the Eucharist cannot approach liturgy as either perfunctory or mechanical, or worse, as a postscript to everything else Franciscans undertake, manipulated to fit whims and fancies. Rather, a Franciscan approach to the Eucharist informs on a very broad scale. It embraces the full ecclesiological dimensions of liturgy with all their corollaries. It is conscious of a full reading of Francis's aims. Thus, it reclaims the spirit of reverence, awe and devotion, attitudes not manufactured but the natural and profound response to an engagement of the sacrament. This is the spirit that informed the early Franciscan movement's celebration of the Eucharist. Franciscans today must offer a wider and more profound experience of Eucharistic enactment. This work of retrieval can be accomplished in a number of ways.

Embrace the Fullness of the Franciscan Tradition

First, the Franciscan family ought to cultivate and embrace a fuller sense of our eight-hundred-year tradition, especially our medieval roots. We as an Order in the Church should not fall into contemporary practices that parcel out segments of the tradition as though they are the fullness of the tradition. We must not succumb to tendencies that would reduce the period between the fourth century and 1963 to a vacuous black hole. Because we are the fruit of a medieval understanding of the cosmos, we must be able to retrieve some aspects of this understanding as they are relevant to contemporary liturgical celebration. We must appreciate the Eucharist as the great and indispensable work of salvation. It is THE work, which helps us understand what it means "to be saved."

Our Franciscan tradition stresses that the Eucharist is an event that both happens to us and acts upon us. Herein lies the center to which every Eucharist gravitates: working to recognize and embrace who and what God is—the "Great Gift-er!"—in the work of creation. The Franciscan Tradition witnesses that attending to liturgy matters; "bad" liturgy is not Franciscan liturgy. If what we do fails to give praise to God and build up the Body of Christ because of a lack of appreciation or effort on our part, then we are short-circuiting the work of redemption.[48]

For this reason, Franciscan eucharistic theology is incompatible with deconstructing liturgy in the interests of simplicity and poverty, especially if these characteristics are understood to emphasize privacy, quietness and an impoverished contemplation. Our tradition reverences and promotes the idea that the fullness of liturgy is the Body of Christ as "a communion gathered and hierarchically ordered." This is not a hierarchy of power and arrogance, but a hierarchy of value and

---

[48] The significance of this activity is expressed every year in the Prayer over the Gifts on Holy Thursday. An English translation of the Latin texts is as follows (italics are mine):
>Lord God,
>make us worthy to celebrate this holy eucharist,
>for as often as this sacrifice is offered
>in remembrance of your Son,
>*the work of our redemption is accomplished.*

dignity of authentic participation. Franciscan teaching on the Eucharist promotes the necessary work of the *full* Body of Christ—all members of the community have a responsibility to contribute in order for the work of salvation to be effective in creation. For Franciscans, the celebration of the Eucharist is a crucial and indispensable Christian "work." It requires us to model for all the faithful a full engagement in this work through authentic and integral enactment!

Retrieve the Sense of Gift and Contingency

Second, the Franciscan community would do well to further retrieve the sense of gift and contingency in Eucharistic celebration. Embracing our tradition assists us in recognizing that an authentic engagement in Eucharist profoundly contributes to what it means to be poor and humble, because through the Eucharist we are called to recognize that without God we are and can do nothing! Such recognition of gift and contingency works to counterbalance a world too often immersed in the pursuit of selfish rights and privileges. Even within the Church, many speak of deserving or having a right to this or that portion of the tradition from all angles and spectrums. How might the Franciscan inspirations of gift and contingency impact such attitudes in the Church and the in world?

Retrieving a fuller sense of gift and contingency in Eucharistic celebration also implies regaining a fuller knowledge of "grace" language in our rites and rituals. For Franciscans, "grace" language is embedded in the concept of sacrament as covenantal encounter: an event, an occasion in which God acts with overwhelming graciousness. Such retrieval places the Eucharist and our engagement unquestionably and principally within the activity of God in history and creation. It further serves to counteract some misinterpretations of Vatican II theology, such as the Eucharist becoming only an event in which we tell our own story or merely a moment in which we say: "Isn't it wonderful for us to be here, God?"[49] The grace language of covenant in and through gift and contingency serves to inform and remind us Franciscans that Eucharist is always directed to God and is not about us.

---

[49] I am indebted to Dr. Kevin Irwin and his course on *Sacramental Treatises*, spring semester 2003, The Catholic University of America, Washington, DC, for these insights. See also Jeremy Driscoll, "The Eucharist and Fundamental Theology," *Ecclesia Orans*, 13 (1996): 407-434.

See Eucharist as Informing Mission

Third, Franciscan Eucharistic theology ought to profoundly inform our sense of mission. At times it appears as if mission is devoted entirely to those tasks, programs and ministries that we Franciscans sponsor or in which we labor. The "tasking" of mission becomes so consuming that liturgy, especially the Eucharist, is seen as an interruption or a disruption of the "real work" of Franciscans. Yet, as Short pointedly remarks, mission is not necessarily in certain activities or speaking a certain message. In actuality, it is the revelation of God through living among others in this good world.[50] Mission must be informed by the Eucharist as a natural progression of its celebration: "Ite, missa est!" or "Go! The Eucharist sends you into the world."

The Eucharist is an *actio* of revelation. Mission must be about revealing who God is. For it to remain truly and uniquely Christian, such work must begin with Eucharist. If our mission as Franciscans does not begin with the Eucharist, it is questionable whether it truly is God's word we proclaim or merely our own. The Eucharist contributed in no small way to Francis's ability to penetrate the vision of creation in heights of contemplation, understanding and service.[51] In following his example, we too are called to penetrate the *actio* of the liturgical event and to attain a higher understanding of our mission as believers in the world.

See Eucharist as Informing Unity

Fourth, an authentic retrieval of the Eucharist must inform the Franciscan commitment to unity in the Church and within the Order. The work of unity is an integral part of our mission as Christian believers. The dual emphasis of the Eucharistic Prayer revolves upon the blessing and transformation of both bread and wine and of those who consume these elements. The principal result of eating and drinking the body and the blood of Christ is a very present, here-and-now focus—the achievement of unity, a unity that is not particular, exclusive, nor anthropocentric, but rather that encompasses all of creation.

The inherent, though at times muted, nature of the Eucharist as a sacrament of unity must have impacted Francis in his conversion and in the elaboration of his mission. The call to repair [a Church] that

---

[50] Short, *The Franciscans*, 129.
[51] Delio, *Franciscan View of Creation*, 6.

was all being destroyed (LMj 2:1) and to "heal the wounded, bind up the broken, and recall the erring" (L3C 58) was a call to recapture and reinvigorate the spirit of unity. From our roots, the quest for unity has been an integral part of our mission as Franciscans—a unity informed by the Eucharist.

The call to build up unity is more than a mission. It must also be witnessed in our own lives as Franciscans. And yet, we must acknowledge that the First Order is divided into Conventual, Capuchin and O.F.M. friars. Such division is the result of neither the intention of Francis nor the discerned inspiration of the Holy Spirit, but a separation that fed upon misunderstandings, misrepresentations and misdirected opinions. It is also a division formalized during a period in which the Reformation was transforming the Church. What witness to the struggle toward unity does such a reality carry with it? If such division within the First Order is maintained, how does it impact a Franciscan theology of Eucharist, whose goal, aim and purpose is to give flesh to the words expressed in the Eucharistic Prayer: *Grant that we, who are nourished by his body and blood, may be filled with his Holy Spirit and become one body, one spirit in Christ* (see Eucharistic Prayer III)?

Recognize Eucharist as Transforming and Healing

Connected with the pursuit of unity is our fifth point: the recognition that engaging in the Eucharist must concern itself with transformation through healing. The Eucharist ought to form Franciscans in our role as ambassadors of reconciliation to those who have lost their way. The fuller meaning of this challenge and responsibility can be discovered through seeing how Francis reflects on the Eucharist and communion. Whenever Francis writes about the Eucharist or Holy Communion, which latter term Francis uses primarily, he emphasizes his desire to remain a part of the Church and does so by affirming the role of clerics in the celebration of the Eucharist. Holy Communion and communion with the greater Body of Christ, the Church, are inseparable for Francis. And yet, the twelfth and thirteenth centuries were not immune to clerical abuse, manipulation, hypocrisy, or a Church attempting to find its way in trying times. In the midst of such turmoil and disenchantment, Francis maintains his faith in the power of the Eucharist and in the Church formed by its grace. He writes most poignantly in *The Testament*: "The Lord gave me, and gives me still, such faith in priests who live according to the rite of the holy Roman Church ... and I desire to respect, love, and honor them ..." (Test 6-9).

Francis's times are indeed not very different from our own as we struggle with a Church betrayed and in need of healing. He offers a challenge to us, and we must wrestle with it in light of our own hardships and disappointments. A Franciscan theology of the Eucharist must always acknowledge Francis's deep love for the Church in all its aspects. As Thomas of Celano wrote: "The first work that blessed Francis undertook ... was to build a house of God. He did not try to build a new one, but he repaired an old one. He did not tear out the foundation, but he built upon it" (1C 18). Francis overcame the limits a blinded Church imposed on access to the Eucharist, yet he never wavered from his committed relationship to, with and for the Church. He devised nothing essentially new, but reconfigured what was so that its impact would reach the faithful. This is the healing we also must be concerned with in our celebration of the Eucharist today.

Recognize Eucharist as Counter-cultural

Sixth and finally, we are called to recognize in the Franciscan perspective on Eucharistic celebration a profoundly counter-cultural stance, revealed as much in the emphasis we place on our need for each other and for communion as it is in the embracing of our Franciscan vows. This position reveals our preference for being over having, for exchange over binding limitations of value, and for the symbolic over the isolating crassness of market mentalities.[52] These are the consequences of being truly formed and informed by what we experience and enact in the Eucharist. Such a realization places the Church and our Order in a unique position of cultural critique and encourages the formation of an alternative to understanding ourselves and our destiny.

Conclusion

These six suggestions are a sample of many ways in which we might reclaim a sense of how Francis and Clare were informed and transformed by the Eucharist. Recognizing the great love of God in the condescension and gift of the Eucharist inspires awe and reverence. The devotion of Francis and Clare allowed the Eucharist to transform

---

[52] See Chauvet, *The Sacraments*, 129-152.

them and then, through them, creation. Francis is one of the first of his time to perceive the great premise of sacramentality, the belief that all creation has the potential to be a revelation of God. Sacramentality serves as a paradigm for all sacramental engagement—experienced most profoundly and intensely in the Eucharist. It is the bridge between the sacred and the secular aspects of human life, drawing us beyond the here and now (see 2Peter 3: 13) to a new heaven and a new earth.[53]

Franciscan Eucharistic theology, therefore, interprets liturgy as enacting the divine and articulating our beliefs. St. Bonaventure saw the world as the book of creation, intended by God to be visible and intelligible to all. However, sin makes this book unintelligible, and so the Father sends the Son, the Wisdom of God and Word of God, to manifest that wisdom in and through the humanity of Jesus Christ. Through knowledge of and imitation of Christ, one comes to know and imitate what is the truth of all reality.[54] Eucharist is for us, as it was for Francis, the principal means to this end. It is not about getting everything right so that it fits within parameters created by our own narrow assessments, but rather about getting life less wrong by letting ourselves be informed and transformed by the challenge and the gift that is the Eucharist!

True Eucharistic theology for Franciscans is then embracing what it means to be eternally catechumens in the ancient sense of the word: those who let sound in our ears and in our very being the divine wisdom of God that echoes through the book of creation. Such eucharistic engagement truly takes to heart what it means to be "learners," as all catechumens are—those contingent human beings beginning ever again "to serve the Lord God, for up until now we have done little or nothing" (1C 103). Adopting this attitude makes us ready to hear and accept readily the Eucharist's gift of divine wisdom and then to let it sound through us—a wisdom based on a relationship of love and gift,[55] hidden through sublime humility and humble sublimity under an ordinary piece of bread (see LtOrd 27).

---

[53] Kevin W. Irwin, "Liturgical *Actio*: Sacramentality, Eschatology and Ecology," in *Contemporary Sacramental Contours of a God Incarnate*, ed. Lieven Boeve and Lambert Leijssen (Leuven: Peeters, 2001), 123.
[54] Delio, *Franciscan View of Creation*, 29-30.
[55] Delio, *Franciscan View of Creation*, 30-31.

CHAPTER FOUR

THE LITURGY OF THE HOURS AND THE RHYTHM OF FRANCISCAN LIFE

William M. Cieslak, O.F.M. Cap.

Introduction

The purpose of this essay is to encourage Franciscans (First Order, Second Order and Third Order secular and regular) to pray the Liturgy of the Hours (as they are able) as part of their daily prayer practice and to do so in a particularly "Franciscan" way.

The Franciscan movement is intended to be a leaven in the world and for the world. It is also a religious movement *in the Church*. It is, by intent, mendicant and itinerant rather than monastic. Franciscanism is a way of living, a spirituality intended for every circumstance of life. For Franciscans, it is not what one *does* that is most important, but *how* one lives and *how* one relates to the people and the world in which one lives.

The spirit of Franciscan living is formed and nurtured in prayer, both private and in common. Prayer concretizes the relationship between God and self, between God and ourselves in community. How we pray, how we address God says something about our understanding of God and our understanding of ourselves. What we pray for serves as a mirror of our deepest concerns and hopes.

St. Francis sought to cultivate in himself a *spirit of prayer* modeled after the spirit of prayer he discovered in the Lord: "No one showed me what I had to do, but the Most High Himself revealed to me that I should live according to the pattern of the Holy Gospel"(Test 14).[1] He sought to imitate Jesus in everything, and prayer was no exception. But his prayer was not simple imitation; his prayer was a true act of

---

[1] All Franciscan sources can be found in *Francis of Assisi: Early Documents*, ed. Regis Armstrong, Wayne Hellmann and William Short, 3 volumes (New York: New City Press, 1999-2001).

love arising from his inner spirit. Prayer celebrated and sealed the relationship Francis had with the Triune God, with Jesus the Christ, with Mary, his Mother, and with all the rest of creation.

Francis's prayer was contemplative.[2] He listened to God speak to him. Francis's prayer was filled with awe as he marveled at the beauty and goodness of creation (CtC). Francis's prayer was filled with praise and thanksgiving, his active response to God's revelation. Francis's prayer was adorational: he responded with reverence to the manifestation of God's love (PrsG; Test 5). Francis's prayer was humble: through his prayer he experienced the Triune God as *humble*. In sending his Son into the world as a fully human creature, limited in space, time and existence, God humbled God's very self! Francis also experienced Jesus' living and dying as one great act of humility (cf. Phil. 2:6-8). Furthermore, Francis was keenly aware of his own sinfulness, of his own creatureliness, of his own complete dependence upon God.[3]

Early accounts testify that Francis prayed the Liturgy of the Hours with all his heart (cf. AC 119-120; 2C 63:96; LMj 8:9, 10:6; 1MP 22, 2MP 7:94). His *Earlier Rule* (1209-1221), *Later Rule* (1223), and *Letter to the Entire Order* (1225-1226) enjoin on all his brothers the recitation of the Liturgy of the Hours as well.[4] From the very beginning, Franciscans have prayed the Liturgy of the Hours with the rest of the Church. The question is not *whether* Francis prayed the Liturgy of the Hours, but *how* he prayed them. Early accounts describe Francis as praying the office with *awe, devotion, joy, peace* and *quiet* (cf. AC 119,120; 2C 62:96). Can we learn to pray in a similar fashion?

In their introduction to Francis's own "office," known today as the *Office of the Passion*, Laurent Gallant, O.F.M., and André Cirino, O.F.M., suggest that Francis prayed this office either as an introduction to the official Liturgy of the Hours or as his spiritual preparation

---

[2] Ilia Delio, O.S.F. *Franciscan Prayer* (Cincinnati: St. Anthony Messenger Press, 2005), 125-143. I am deeply indebted to Delio for her fine treatment of Franciscan prayer. This work serves as a major foundation for my essay.

[3] Delio devotes a chapter of her book on "Learning to Gaze: Poverty and Prayer." In gazing upon God, Francis and Clare recognized their own poverty in relation to God, but they also discovered God's own humility in relation to themselves and all human beings. See Delio, 77-90.

[4] The *Earlier Rule*, chapter 3, also enjoins on the brothers who could not read, the praying of the Creed, Our Father and Doxology, in various combinations and repetitions, for each of the canonical hours. In the *Later Rule*, chapter 3, only the repetition of the Our Father is mentioned for those who cannot read.

for celebrating them.⁵ The *Office of the Passion* contains a set of fifteen original "psalms," each set within a larger prayer format. Each can be used interchangeably to mark the liturgical hours of the day, the week and the liturgical season. Perhaps this office gives an insight into Francis's spirituality and a Franciscan approach to the Liturgy of the Hours.

Methodology

The first presupposition of this essay is that there are particular characteristics to Franciscan prayer that we can locate within the spiritual-theological-intellectual tradition. The second presupposition is that these characteristics color the way Franciscans pray the Liturgy of the Hours.

We begin by describing several of these characteristics found in our spiritual-intellectual tradition, including the *Office of the Passion*. We then describe the Liturgy of the Hours as a communal prayer event in the Church and the principles that serve as the foundation of this prayer. Our third task will be to relate the pattern of Franciscan living to the general pattern of the Liturgy of the Hours. Finally, we will pay some attention to the creativity of St. Francis as found in his *Office of the Passion* and suggest how similar creativity might be applied to a communal Franciscan celebration of Morning and Evening Prayer.

Characteristics of Franciscan Prayer

The Franciscan "characteristics" presented below could have been grouped and identified in many other ways. Note, too, that the "characteristics" presented are inter-connected and that they inter-mingle. One might even consider the various characteristics as dimensions of an over-arching *attitude of the heart at prayer*. In prayer, words lose their specificity and precision.

1. *Franciscan prayer begins in the heart, not the head. It is CONTEMPLATIVE in a very receptive way.*

Awareness is the first movement of Franciscan prayer.⁶ It begins with an attitude of openness and availability towards God and towards

---
⁵ *The Geste of the Great King: Office of the Passion of St. Francis of Assisi*, ed. Laurent Gallant, O.F.M., and André Cirino, O.F.M. (St. Bonaventure, NY: The Franciscan Institute, 2001).

⁶ See especially chapters four and seven of Delio , 75-90, 125-143.

God's desire to speak with us. Contemplation includes our invitation to God to speak with us. If we want to enter into relationship, we must make relationship possible. We must make room for it by clearing out our own desires to speak first and our own agendas. This means *developing a listening attitude*, patiently waiting, eagerly waiting. This accompanying-waiting is faith-filled, confident invocation, inviting THE OTHER to be present. Jesus promised, "Where two or three are gathered together in my name, there am I in the midst of them" (Mt. 18:20).

Receiving or welcoming God is the second movement. With our welcome, relationship happens. Since GOD is LOVE (1John 4:16), when love greets us and we welcome love in return, love happens! The event is an event of the heart, not of the head. The purpose of waiting in hope and faith is to RECEIVE the OTHER as person and not as object, that is, in the *heart*. It is not merely to become aware of the other or to receive some information about the other. The verb, "to contemplate," might seem like a call from the mind to think about some object, but in Franciscan prayer, it is a call from the heart to greet the other as person and not as object. Contemplation means being in the presence of the BELOVED, being with the BELOVED.

2. *Franciscan prayer begins with a humble acknowledgement of who we humans are in relation to the all good, all loving, creating TRIUNE GOD. It is ADORATIONAL.*

The prophet Isaiah stammers out his response upon experiencing God: "Woe is me, I am doomed! For I am a man of unclean lips, living among a people of unclean lips; yet my eyes have seen the King, the Lord of hosts!" (Is. 6:5). In God's holy presence, we human beings sense our unworthiness. God who made us and who sustains our lives in being is so much greater than we ourselves. In the act of contemplation we see God in perspective. God is the One who IS, and we are mere creatures who need not be! God is the One who is LOVE and who loves each of us first, before we do anything (2LtF 18). The experience of this is deeply humbling.

But being loved by any other human being is deeply humbling as well. The love of the beloved is true gift, free gift, incomparable gift.

It fixes my attention on the "other" and off myself. It is, in some way, adorational.[7] How much more so with GOD!

Human language fails in two ways with regard to contemplation: human language is not adequate to express the love of two human beings for each other. It is even more inadequate to express God's holy relationship with us. Human words, human gestures, human sounds, even silence, offer no adequate communication with or description of the Beloved *with* us. All of our responses are inadequate to the experience. And yet, we must try.[8]

In Franciscan theology, God is GOOD, God is LOVE, God is TRIUNE, God is FREE, God is NECESSARY and God is HUMBLE.[9] Everything that is, every created being in the universe, is created in God's image and through God's love. Jesus, in turn, is the first born of all creation, the ultimate gift of the Triune God.[10] Jesus is the Word of God incarnate. Everything is created through him. Every living thing is "good." Every living thing participates in the living presence of God and reveals something of God.

God creates freely. God creates *because* God is good and overflowing with love. God, as all good and all loving, God as Trinity of persons in love, is the foundational reason for all creation, for everything that is. Everything that is is held in existence by God, and God is manifest in everything. This is a deeply Franciscan understanding.

What is more, God reveals Godself as present to us human creatures. God empties Godself to be present in a way we can receive. God humbles Godself to be present to us in a way we can apprehend. Francis recognized this as he contemplated the mystery of the Incarnation. He discovered the humility of God in gazing upon God and in gazing upon Jesus.

---

[7] In love, the beloved often feels unworthy of the love of the other. This sense of unworthiness in the presence of the other can lead the beloved to "worship" or "adore" the other, humanly speaking.

[8] This human inability to respond adequately to God in words is the basic reason why Franciscan prayer focuses more on the attitude of the praying spirit than on the words used in the prayer.

[9] See especially Delio, chapters five, six and seven.

[10] In the blessing of the Easter candle during the Easter Vigil service Christ is proclaimed: "Christ, yesterday and today/ the beginning and the end/ Alpha/ and Omega/ all time belongs to him/ and all the ages/ to him be glory and power/ through every age forever." And in the Nicene Creed we profess: "Through him all things were made."

3. *Franciscan prayer acknowledges who we humans are in relation to God and in relation to the rest of creation. It is filled with PRAISE AND THANKSGIVING.*

Because of God's innate and overwhelming goodness and love, everything that is invites the believer to *praise and thank* God. Because God creates, God is praised and thanked. Thus, along with adoration and a deep sense of being loved, the Franciscan responds with praise, blessing and thanksgiving, just as Mary did ("My soul proclaims the greatness of the Lord; my spirit rejoices in God my savior"[Lk. 1:46]) and as Zachary did ("Blessed be the Lord, the God of Israel, for he has visited and brought redemption to his people" [Lk. 1:68]). This is the appropriate response to the saving presence of God in our midst.

The attitude of *praise or blessing* responds to the awareness of God's deep, abiding, pulsing, living presence. The attitude of praise receives the goodness and love of God and acknowledges it. Such an attitude becomes *cosmic* as we realize that every bit of creation is a gift and sacrament of God and that we ourselves are part of this creation, part of the fabric of created being. In this world everything is *related* to everything else. When we further realize that the human voice can offer praise and blessing on behalf of every created thing, we understand that our prayer of praise is offered in the name of all. Our prayer of praise and blessing, while always creaturely, is yet cosmic at the same time. It acknowledges that God is God and we are not!

Thanksgiving is the next breath. Peter, James and John uttered their thanksgiving at the transfiguration of Jesus: "Lord, it is good that we are here" (Mt. 17:4). Simeon proclaimed his thanksgiving after seeing the Lord: "Now, Master, you may let your servant go in peace, according to your word, for my own eyes have seen your salvation" (Lk. 2:29-30). Mary Magdalene, the disciples on the road to Emmaus, the apostles in the upper room were all filled with awe and gratitude, excitement and joy at seeing the Lord. Is there any doubt that eucharist (from the Greek, meaning thanksgiving) for the living-dying-rising of Jesus would become the weekly Christian response. "Let us give thanks to the Lord, our God."[11]

We give thanks because God is with us, because God's presence is gift freely given. We give thanks because in God we are sustained. We give thanks because Love loves us! We give thanks because it is right and just to do so.

---

[11] From the opening dialogue to the Eucharistic prayer.

If the act of contemplation opens us to the indwelling of God, not only within us but also around us and beside us and through us, praise and thanksgiving are the creaturely stammers, the human "Amen" to God's power and goodness and love.

4. *Franciscan prayer is Christocentric in its language, addressed to the Triune God and graced by the Spirit.*

We often think of Franciscan prayer as being *simply* Christocentric. This is not the case, at least not in the prayer of Francis and Clare.[12] Because Jesus is the incarnation of God and because he is the firstborn of every creature, Jesus is the human vehicle, the ground sacrament, for everything else.[13] But it is of the nature of sacrament to point beyond itself to God; and this is precisely what Jesus does for Francis and Clare. They do not treat Jesus as the center of their lives; they treat Jesus as the WAY to *communion* with the TRIUNE GOD.

John's Gospel, a favorite of Francis, points out again and again that Jesus is the WAY to the Father.[14] The clearest, surest way we can know God is through Jesus. Friendship with Jesus is friendship with God through Jesus. The nativity of Jesus and the crucifixion are two important icons of the love of the Triune God. Both icons lead to God; both manifest the awesome humility of God-for-us!

5. *Franciscan prayer is spiritual communion marked by God's goodness, love, holiness, peace and joy.*

The new themes here are *peace* and *joy*. Communion in God and with God ushers in peace[15] and joy as well. These are effects of communion in God's creating goodness and love. Franciscan spirituality is marked by peace and joy, not in any superficial or casual way, but at the core of presence with God. Julian of Speyer, in his life of St. Francis, cites joy as the power of the presence of God in Francis that enabled him to lead a converted way of life, independent from what others thought or said (LJS 1:7). It also caused him to greet others with the familiar Franciscan phrase: "May the Lord give you peace"(LJS 3:16).

---

[12] Delio says as much in her chapter, "Friendship with Christ," 91-106.

[13] For more on the Franciscan understanding of the role of Christ see *Franciscan Christology*, ed. Damian McElrath, (St. Bonaventure, NY: The Franciscan Institute, 1980).

[14] Cf. John 4:34; 5:19-30; 5:36-40; 5:43; 7:16; 8:16-19; 8:38; 10:14-18; 10:25-38; 12:49-50; 14:6-14; 14:20-30; 15:1-17; 16:23-28; 17:1-26.

[15] Delio dedicates a chapter to peace, 165-180.

It is one thing to experience peace or joy *around* oneself or *between* oneself and others. To experience peace and joy *within* oneself, as the result of communion with God, is a much deeper experience, not dependent on external relationships but on interior communion. Nothing from the outside can destroy it. Franciscan peace and joy, therefore, are deep qualities of a life lived in the Spirit of God.

6. *Franciscan prayer involves silence, beauty, sound, smell, taste; it involves the body and all the senses. It is* SACRAMENTAL.

One might find the use of the word "sacramental" in the above statement surprising. Sacramental in this sense refers to the visible, tangible dimension of life as bearing the holy. Franciscan prayer takes seriously the created world, not in a generic way but in its particularity and specificity. Each individual being bears something of the holy and communicates the holy in some particular, specific way. Beautiful things especially communicate something of the goodness of God. Beautiful things, therefore, can lead us all into prayer.

For human beings, communion with God involves our bodies, our senses and the material world around us in which we are immersed. We do not pray with our minds alone, but through our bodies, which are the means through which God speaks with us and is present to us. Our bodies are also the means through which we pray, adore, communicate, praise, thank and implore. The mystery of the Incarnation is revealed in the concrete universe, and the prayer of us humans is taken up into the Incarnation of God. In the Franciscan framework, every thing matters!

Characteristics of the Church's Liturgy of the Hours

The practice of the celebration of the Liturgy of the Hours developed gradually in the early Church. The inspiration for this prayer form is Jesus' own example of praying constantly, his request to his disciples that they pray (Lk. 18:1) and Paul's request to the Thessalonian community to pray constantly (1Thess. 5:17).[16]

---

[16] Note, for example, the number of times that Jesus is seen at prayer in Luke's gospel. See also, Sacred Congregation for Divine Worship, "General Instruction of the Liturgy of the Hours," 2 Feb., 1972, 1.3; 2:5.

1. *The purpose behind the Liturgy of the Hours is to mirror Jesus' life. He prayed always.*

The pattern that gradually evolved into the various "hours" that constitute the Church's official Liturgy of the Hours arose in response to the practice in Jesus' life of praying constantly and in his command to pray always. The pattern developed differently among urban Christians, who gathered in the central city churches (later called cathedrals) in the morning and in the evening, and among the monks, who gathered in their respective monastic communities to dot the day and night with prayer and reflection. While there was one injunction, there were two different models, each dependent on concrete circumstances and limitations. While these two models have been classically called "cathedral" and "monastic," I will call them "popular" and "monastic," referring to the particular community of believers who assembled, rather than to the location in which they prayed. Some of the suggestions I present are dependent on this shift.

Whether a group of monks or a group of urban Christians, the result is a community of believers gathered in the name of Jesus, praying day and night, celebrating their Christian discipleship, renewing and enriching their faith, energizing themselves to continue following the Way, the Truth and the Life.

The monks, having more free time and living in close proximity to a chapel, could divide their day into seven distinct "hours." They rose in the middle of the night to pray Matins. They prayed Lauds at sunrise, Terce at nine in the morning, Sext at noon, None at three in the afternoon. They celebrated Vespers as the sun began to set. Compline served as their night prayer before going to bed. The monks gathered around great hand-lettered psalters and read in common, using all one hundred and fifty psalms of the Old Testament. The form of this prayer is characterized as "edificational" or faith-building, since the full use of the one hundred and fifty psalms was meant to inspire or "build up," enrich and enlarge the hearts of the monks praying.

The town-folk, on the other hand, committed to making a living, began the day with morning prayer and ended it with evening prayer. Without electricity, social life was simple. The day began with sunrise and ended with nightfall. Without Xerox copies, the people sang refrains to a few well-known psalms, suitable for the morning or the evening. They entered into the rhythm of the prayer through bodily gestures and postures, through song and silence, through sight and smell. The form of this prayer was popular and the content was devotional. Its purpose was to keep the living-dying-rising of Jesus in the hearts and on the lips of the worshippers. It provided them with a repeatable ritual and songs and prayers they could memorize. They experienced the power of communal praying; their faith was nourished through sitting, standing, singing, praying together.

Each form of prayer fulfilled, in its own ways, the command of Christ to pray always. Each was created out of the particular living situations of the Christians who gathered to pray. Each was dependant on the resources at hand and the creativity of those who oversaw the communal prayer life.

2. *The Liturgy of the Hours is an act of Christ and his Church: the Priestly People of God join in communion through, with and in Christ.*

Jesus Christ, as the unique great high priest (Heb. 4:14) seated at the right hand of the Father, prays continuously for the world (Heb. 8:1). In the Liturgy of the Hours, the baptized faithful, as part of the priesthood of all believers by reason of our holy baptism, enter into this prayer of Christ. "As we celebrate the office, therefore, we must recognize our own voices echoing in Christ, his voice echoing in us."[17] We join in the priestly prayer of Christ. We pray in his holy presence, through communion with his Paschal Mystery. Through our prayer in Christ, we become the Body of Christ, praying with Christ our head.

Praying the Liturgy of the Hours, while required of all in holy orders, is nevertheless a "priestly" exercise of all of the baptized as well. In holy baptism we are swept up into the mystery of Christ, his Paschal Mystery. We were buried with him so that, "just as Christ was raised from the dead by the glory of the Father, we too might live in newness of life" (Rom. 6:4). Because of this grace we all have a role in the priestly praying of Christ for the world. Even though the baptized have no individual obligation to celebrate the Liturgy of the Hours, we have the *right* to celebrate it. When we make use of this right, we realize our baptismal role as God's holy people and our participation in Christ's mission to the world.

---

[17] Pope Paul VI, *Laudis Canticum*, 1 Nov., 1970, International Commission on English in the Liturgy, *Documents on the Liturgy: 1963-1979* (Collegeville, MN: The Liturgical Press, 1982), 1089. The passage refers to Augustine, *Enarrat. In Ps. 85*, I: *Corpus Christianorum Series latina* 39, 1176.

3. The Liturgy of the Hours also "remembers" the Paschal Mystery of Jesus.

As is true of all liturgical prayer, the celebration of the Liturgy of the Hours focuses on the Paschal Mystery of Jesus, his life lived in obedience, his sufferings and eventual death on a cross out of love for us all, his resurrection and ascension to God's right hand and his continual intercession for us in heaven. This is the baptism into which we were baptized. It is the anointed life into which we have been confirmed. It is the life that sustains, nourishes, heals and builds us up every time we celebrate the Eucharist. It is the life of prayerful communion that helps us live every moment of every day. The liturgical life of the Church is never play-acting nor merely remembering what happened to Jesus in the past. Liturgy involves a special kind of remembering, an active-dynamic-self-involving remembering that transforms our lives into the heart of the mystery of Jesus, the once-for-all and once-for-everyone abundant life of Christ.

The Liturgy of the Hours does this by taking time seriously. It takes the time of day and relates that to the Paschal Mystery of Jesus *through the ritual*, a combination of songs, hymns, psalms, Scriptural passages and other texts, through posture, place, gestures, music, silence and time. For example, Lauds, or morning prayer, prayed as the sun rises and the new day begins, celebrates the resurrection of Jesus. Vespers, or evening prayer, prayed as the sunlight fades and darkness comes upon the earth, celebrates the death of Jesus. Thus remembrance-celebration of the Paschal Mystery of Jesus, the dying and rising of the Lord, is the daily occurrence, the daily pattern of Christians as we seek to allow the Lord to transform our lives and use them for the completion of his mission.

4. The Liturgy of the Hours takes the time of day seriously.

It is still the practice of some clerics, bound to the obligation of praying the Liturgy of the Hours, to sit once a day and "pray" all of the "hours" one after the other.[18] While this practice may fulfill most of the letter

---

[18] Reciting the entire Office was the prescript for all in major orders. As a result, it was essential to recite all of the hours each and every day. Due to individual work schedules, this often led to sitting down once or twice a day and "saying" large portions of the office. After Vatican Council II, the Church re-defined the Liturgy of the Hours. The hour of Prime was suppressed. Terce, Sext, or None could be said, depending on the hour of the day at which it was said. Lauds and Vespers came to be seen as the chief hours, the "two hinges on which the daily office turns." (Vatican Council II,

of the law, it does not fulfill the spirit. Each hour of the liturgy, with the exception of the Office of Readings, Matins, is meant to be prayed at the appropriate time during the day. Each hour no longer has the same value: of all the hours, Lauds and Vespers, morning and evening prayer, are of prime importance in the daily rhythm of life. These are the "hinge hours" on which the rest of the Liturgy of the Hours rests, the foundational hours, the special hours. These hours mark the beginning and ending of the day.

Each hour has its own proper character, each participates in the Paschal Mystery in its own particular way. Morning prayer begins the new day, thanks God for creation and celebrates the Resurrection of the Lord. Evening prayer ends the daylight, reviews the day and offers sorrow for sin, remembers those of have died and celebrates the Death of the Lord. Thus in the two are the central Mysteries of Christ celebrated as well as central devotional expressions of praise/thanksgiving and repentance. "From the rising of the sun to its setting is the name of the Lord to be praised" (Ps. 113 [112]). Compline, the night prayer of the Church, asks God to protect us through the night and prays for a happy death. Terce and Sext are the daytime prayers, from which one may choose. Matins, the hour that focuses on select readings for the feast or season, plays its own particular role and can be prayed at any time.

5. *The Liturgy of the Hours not only sanctifies the day, but also sanctifies the whole range of human activity.*[19]

Morning prayer consecrates the day, asks God to be with us in all we do and sets before us the goals and focus of our actions. Daytime prayer causes us to pause and reflect on what we are doing and how we are living the day. Evening prayer looks back on the day, thanking God for the ways God has blessed us and the work of our hands, asking for forgiveness for those things we could have done better. Night prayer asks God to watch over us as we sleep and entrusts our sleep to God. These times of prayer call God to be a constant part of our lives and call us to God. They motivate us to do what we do

---

Sacrosanctum Concilium, 4 Dec., 1963, no. 89.a.) The General Instruction on the Liturgy of the Hours changed the obligation of praying the office. While those in sacred orders "should" pray the full sequence of hours each day, they "should not omit except for a serious reason" the two hinges of the liturgy of the hours, morning and evening prayer (no. 29).

[19] SCDW, "General Instruction on the Liturgy of the Hours," 2 February, 1971, no. 11.

in the best way possible. They encourage patience and perseverance. They also remind us that the world does not revolve around us, but that our world revolves around God—God is the center and we are not. Praying the hours reminds us that we are part of a much larger universe and that how we live in that universe affects the whole of it.

6. *The Liturgy of the Hours gives us a steady daily structure for living and serves as a constant reminder of who we are in Christ.*

By beginning each day with praise and thanksgiving, we remind ourselves that we live constantly in the presence of God, not just when we think about it. The hours call us into God's presence, reminding us that God is first and central. Like a uniform that one wears to remind oneself of one's role or one's responsibilities, the Liturgy of the Hours informs us who we really are, God's creation, and how we are to live and conduct ourselves as Christ's baptized and consecrated people. By pausing in our life and work, we are called back to our life-giving center, redirected and renewed in our purpose. It is more difficult to wander far from God when one stays faithful to this way of prayer.

We also begin to realize that God is the one who is working through us, and our achievements are not our own. Little by little, with faithful practice, our lives are transformed into the Christian life we claim is our identity.

The Pattern of Franciscan Living and the Liturgy of the Hours

Because most Franciscans live and work in the world rather than in a cloistered situation, attention needs to be given to relating the pattern of prayer of the Liturgy of the Hours to the lifestyles of Franciscans. Most Franciscans living and working in the United States are not bound to celebrate the Liturgy of the Hours in its entirety or even in its official form. Thus, a great deal of flexibility and creativity are possible.[20] How can our prayer be adapted to enable it to be more Franciscan?

---

[20] Only those Franciscans in holy orders are bound to the celebration of the entire course of the Liturgy of the Hours in its official form, and even here, as noted above, there is some flexibility. The rest of the Franciscan family enjoys a great deal of flexibility and creativity in celebrating hours of the Liturgy of the Hours. Thus, the purpose of this essay.

The Franciscan movement is located within the Church. In fact, when one totals up all the Franciscans of the First, Second and Third Orders (secular and regular), as well as others who feel called to share in our Franciscan spirituality, it is obvious that the Franciscan movement is one of the larger spiritual movements in the Church. Thus, Franciscans seek to pray with the rest of the universal Church precisely because we are Franciscan. Francis and Clare of Assisi always sought to pray *in* the Church. They valued the approval of the Church for their rules of life and always saw themselves as totally within the mantle of the Church.

Franciscans also value community and prayer in common. Franciscan spirituality is essentially relational; it is about relationships between God and ourselves, among ourselves and between humans and the rest of the created universe. If our spirituality is communal, so our prayer life must be as communal as possible.[21]

The *Constitution on the Sacred Liturgy* states that since liturgy by its nature is communal, the communal form of celebration has precedence over private celebration.[22] A difficulty arises with regard to using the official breviary book communally. It was published with only meager musical choices and few communal references. Although, since Vatican Council II, the practice has arisen of reciting the Liturgy of the Hours using the breviary in common, many communities of monks, whose lives incorporate the full celebration of the Liturgy of the Hours, celebrate those hours in their full musical form. Therefore, they must use other printed sources, more conducive to communal celebration.

Since Franciscans do not live in monasteries, since Franciscans desire communal prayer, and since Franciscans invite lay people into their prayer, perhaps we would benefit from a more *popular* form of the Liturgy of the Hours. We might borrow from the old cathedral (popular) practices with a simpler content and more musical form. In developing new ways of praying the Liturgy of the Hours, Franciscans need to keep the following issues in mind. The prayer should strive to

- be faithful to the spirit of the official Liturgy of the Hours;
- be prayed communally;

---

[21] Just how communal should it be? Should local communities of friars and sisters invite others into our common prayer?

[22] Vatican Council II, *Sacrosanctum Concilium*, no. 27. Regarding the communal celebration of the Liturgy of the Hours in particular, see SCDW, General Instruction of the Liturgy of the Hours, no. 33.

- be prayed at times that fit with the requirements of ministry in the world;
- invite and attract Christians living in the world;
- be celebrated in a manner that reflects the Franciscan spirit of prayer;
- invite those who pray into close relationship with God, each other and all the rest of creation.

Toward a Franciscan Way of Praying the Liturgy of the Hours in the world

In addition to praying the Liturgy of Hours of the Roman Church, Francis prayed *The Office of the Passion,* which he himself composed. This marvelous work gives us an insight into Francis's own spirit. While following the practice of praying seven times a day, the *Office* is actually composed of fifteen "psalms," the "Our Father" and the short doxology, the "Praises to be said at all the Hours," the "Antiphon of Mary," and the Blessing-Dismissal. The psalms are so arranged that different combinations of them can be used for various times of the day, for various feasts and during various liturgical seasons.

What is most fascinating is how Francis composed the "psalms" and the other created texts. The "psalms" are made up of phrases from the Old Testament psalms themselves and from other Scriptural phrases—phrases that "stuck" to Francis's own heart.[23] Francis, in experiencing the oral celebration of the Liturgy of the Hours, heard and carried words and phrases from it in his heart. The "Praises to be said at all the Hours," however, begins with phrases from the Book of Revelation (Rev. 4:8, 4:11, 5:11) and then transposes to segments from the Canticle of Daniel (3:57, 85).

Francis's heart clearly was open to the world around him, its needs and challenges. His heart was formed by a certain attitude towards God and a clarity about how God revealed Godself and how Christ revealed himself. The "dialogue" that ensued between Francis and the world and between Francis and the Triune God is the "stuff" of the *Office of the Passion.* The Office is a way of viewing life, a way of acknowledging the influence and power of God and of Christ in

---

[23] Phrases from Psalm 9, 13, 17, 18, 20, 22, 31, 34, 35, 38, 41, 42, 44, 46, 47, 56, 57, 59, 66, 68, 69, 70, 71, 72, 73, 74, 75, 81, 86, 88, 89, 96, 98, 109, 118, 136, 142, 144. Scriptural phrases are from Ex. 15:2, Ex. 15:6-7, Is. 9:6, Is. 12:1, Is. 12:2, Lam. 1:12, Sir. 51,1, Mt. 11:25, Mt. 16:24, Mt. 17:5, Mt. 26:42, Lk. 1:68, Lk. 2:7, Lk. 2:14, Lk. 14: 27, Jn. 8:17, Jn. 17:11, Jn. 19:7, Gal. 4:4, 1Th. 1:9, Heb. 9:12, 1Jn. 4:9, 1Jn. 5:7, 1Pt. 2:21.

Francis's life, a way of bringing "the world" in which he lived into his prayer and a way of receiving strength, direction and comfort for his own life and ministry.

This attention to the presence of God, this attention to the needs of his heart, this attention to the situation in which he lived served as the "matter" for his composition. It also serves as an inspiration for Franciscan praying today. Perhaps it is this that enabled Francis to "pray" the Liturgy of the Hours with full devotion and joy.

Some Suggestions

1. Because Franciscan praying has more to do with the heart than the mind, the form of the prayer is less important than the attitude of prayer.

Because Franciscan prayer seeks to be contemplative, adorational, cosmic and joyful, prayer must begin in a Franciscan frame of mind. The spirit must be quieted, the ears must listen to hear God's voice and welcome God's faithful presence. The eyes must be opened to see God's presence everywhere, and the heart must be stretched to love all of creation. The voice must be freed to sing our praise and thanks and that of all creation. And as the all-good and loving God reveals Godself through the presence of the humble Christ, the Spirit of God will raise us up and give us new life and energy to continue the saving work of Jesus on earth. Time and effort have to be given to this before communal prayer begins.

A way to accomplish this might be to create a pattern for entering into common prayer, a pattern that would include some adorational gesture, ample silence, clearing the mind of concerns, developing a listening attitude, entering into communion with the rest of creation and an invitation to Christ to be present.

In the course of the prayer, the heart would welcome the voice of God heard in the psalm texts and in the hymns, in the music and in the environment that encompasses the prayer. God's presence would be seen in the faces of those who are present and in the remembrance of those who are absent. The words sung and spoken, the silences observed, would become the "words" of the communion taking place with God. The intercessions, at the end of the prayer, would swell the heart, expanding it to the breadth, height and depth of Christ's own heart. The result would be a deeper, richer way of praying the Liturgy of the Hours in common. It could effect in us what Francis's biographers saw happen in him.

2. In general, morning and evening would be the central times for prayer.

The Liturgy of the Hours for Franciscans might center each day around the celebration of morning and evening prayer. This simple prayer pattern would leave ample time for ministry in the world. Praying the hours would form in the community of believers a richer Franciscan spirit.

The beginning of a new day calls us to communion with the rest of creation. The world is filled with the sounds of life waking up. The sun changes color and rises to rouse us from sleep. We realize that, like all the rest, we too are creatures. But we have human spirits and minds and voices. We can gather in groups and raise our voices in common prayer and sing praise in the name of all. God becomes wonderfully present through an attitude of praise and thanksgiving. Everything present is brought into the divine dialogue, without concern for control or order or logic. The agenda for the day is placed in God's presence to be transformed. Through centering on Christ and his Paschal Mystery, those praying gain power to witness and minister, strength to overcome the day's obstacles and focus to bring to the task. Joy, love and peace, generated in this time of prayer, are gratefully shared.

The end of the day, sunset, works in reverse. The sun retreats into the western sky and grows pale. But the moon, the planets and the stars appear, as sentinels of the night. Creatures burst out in song. Our own bodies have grown weary and hungry with the work of the day. We gather again and praise God for another day, for used and unused opportunities, and we unite ourselves to the sufferings and death of the Lord Jesus—a reminder that God is love, that God is good.

We bring the successes of the day to our prayer and the failures as well. We come into the presence of the Lord and allow the Lord to minister to us. We experience God's goodness and love and settle in to praise. We remember that we are creatures, not God, and, despite what has happened during the course of the day, we are good and we are loved.

3. The content of the prayer would derive from the content of the Liturgy of the Hours, from the Scripture that "sticks" to the heart, from the songs and hymns that help the heart sing praise and thanks, from the dialogue that takes place between the all-good, all loving triune God and ourselves, and from the dialogue that takes place between ourselves and the rest of the world we serve.

The content of the prayer needs to inspire us to love more deeply and more broadly. It needs to strengthen our resolve to serve the Lord in a world that does not understand. It needs to open our eyes to the poor and powerless and welcome them into our lives. It needs to gird us in peace and patience. It needs to help us find words of sorrow when we fail to live life in abundance and to help us ask for forgiveness when we do wrong.

The form of the prayer, although a secondary concern, must nevertheless create a communal experience for the worshippers. By choosing musical settings, psalm texts and readings that move, melt and expand the heart, we may achieve an effective sense of community.

The way the Hours are celebrated must demonstrate passion and urgency, honesty and devotion. "Good celebrations foster and nourish faith. Poor celebrations may weaken and destroy it."[24] Thus we must ask: What are the gestures that nourish and express faith? What are the musical psalms that fill the heart with awe or sorrow or joy or adoration or repentance? How can we create a pattern for prayer that people can own as their own and use fully without getting bored?

Conclusion

Little attention has been given in the past to the relationship between liturgy and Franciscan spirituality, let alone the Liturgy of the Hours and our Franciscan life. We would do well, now, to develop a Franciscan attitude toward praying the Liturgy of the Hours. Then, out of that attitude, we must begin to attend to how God is speaking to us and what is moving and forming our hearts. We must also look to the needs of our sisters and brothers in faith and ask the questions: "What will help us all pray with a more lively, impassioned spirit?" "What will give us the courage to live the kinds of gospel lives the Lord is calling us to?"

Francis created his *Office of the Passion* over time. He collected the psalm fragments and other phrases from the Sacred Scriptures in his heart. He chose a form, the *geste*, in which to create his praises. He used this *Office* to assist his own prayer and prayed it in his own social, cultural, personal context. Our task is not to imitate his *Office*, but to create one for our own times and circumstances.

---

[24] United States Conference of Catholic Bishops, "Music in Catholic Worship," (1972), no. 6.

Life without liturgy has a shallow foundation and little direction. Liturgy, out of step with life, is doomed to die because it is not being fed by the stuff of daily life. Discovering the relationship between the two is worth every bit of the effort!

CHAPTER FIVE

FRANCISCAN DEVOTIONS AND POSTMODERN CULTURE

Daniel P. Grigassy, O.F.M.

Introduction

At the time of the eight-hundredth anniversary of the birth of St. Francis in 1982, nine friars minor in the United States formed a group that called themselves the Committee for Franciscan Liturgical Research (CFLR). They produced a sizeable book titled *Franciscans at Prayer* made up of nine chapters, including common texts and litanies, private prayers, prayers for a chapter, special times of prayer, prayers in sickness and death, devotions, blessings, selected psalms and canticles, and hymnody.[1] Paragraph 5 of the collection (there are no page numbers) states:

> The present (1983) edition of *Franciscans at Prayer* is being prepared for the members of the Order of Friars Minor in North America for their private use for a period of five years. During that time the Committee for Franciscan Liturgical Research hopes to test the selection of prayers and the usefulness of the devotions contained in the book. As more friars become aware of the book and of the ongoing project to revise it, friars will bring to the attention of the CFLR other devotions, prayers, and hymns which ought to be included.

Five years later, in 1988, no word was heard from the Committee on a revision of the book. We are still waiting. Franciscans would rather engage the marketplace in popular preaching and evangelization than revise a liturgical book.

---

[1] *Franciscans at Prayer* (Pulaski, WI: Franciscan Publishers, 1983).

On Holy Thursday 1992, the Italian text of a pastoral letter was issued by the ministers general of the Franciscan Families titled "On Liturgical Life." It was published in *Acta Ordinis Fratrum Minorum*[2] and the English text followed soon thereafter in *Greyfriars Review*.[3] *The Cord* reprinted the pastoral letter[4] followed by four commentaries by friars from each of the Order's branches (O.F.M., O.F.M. Conv., O.F.M. Cap., and T.O.R.), representing the general ministers who authored it. At the time of preparing the issue, we thought it would become a prime source of reflection and a catalyst for discussion in local communities. In the months and years that followed, to my knowledge, the pastoral letter was never discussed. The issue of *The Cord* did not stimulate discussion. Franciscans would rather engage the marketplace in popular preaching and evangelization than discuss and debate a pastoral letter from their leaders.

Franciscans have never been associated with things liturgical as the Benedictines have been. Nor have the Jesuits. More comfortable in the library than in the sanctuary, Jesuits before the liturgical reform and renewal of the last forty years were caricatured as fumbling through the Missal, desperately trying to figure out what came next. The old expression, "Lost as a Jesuit in Holy Week," told the story. An effective Jesuit liturgy has been described as a religious rite "when no one gets hurt."[5]

Before, during and after Vatican II, some formidable liturgical scholars and practitioners emerged from the Society of Jesus. In June 2002, over 120 Jesuits gathered in Rome from forty-two countries for a week of deliberation on the role of liturgy. Twenty non-Jesuit collaborators joined them. The Jesuit superior general desired the scope of the symposium to be broadened beyond Jesuit life and mission to ways in which the Society might put its life and membership at the service of the Church.

Franciscans would not have a symposium on the role of liturgy in their life or in the life of the Church—up to this moment! I am delighted that the title of this year's Franciscan Symposium at the Washington Theological Union is "Let Us Praise, Adore and Give Thanks: Franciscans and Liturgical Life." May it be the first of many such symposia!

---

[2] *Acta Ordinis Fratrum Minorum* 111.2 (1992): 85-93.
[3] *Greyfriars Review* 6.3 (1992): 267-278.
[4] *The Cord* 43.6 (1993): 162-169.
[5] Keith F. Pecklers, S.J., ed., *Liturgy in a Postmodern World* (New York: Continuum, 2003), 2.

The title that was assigned to me was "Franciscan Devotions and Postmodern Culture." First, I will attend to that slippery term "postmodern" and come to some understanding of it. Then I want to consider the phenomena of devotions unique to our Franciscan tradition within "a" postmodern culture, that of America, viz., North America, perhaps only the eastern, or more particularly, the northeastern part of the United States, and then reflect theologically on the phenomena. Since it is true that "all theology is local," I can reflect theologically only on what is experienced in my locale, viz., the northeastern axis, from Boston to Washington, DC, where I have lived most of my life.

Postmodern

Throughout the 1990s, hundreds if not thousands of books and articles were published in this country with some form of the word "postmodern" in the title. It was the buzzword. Acknowledgments of the term's colluded definitions and confusion of meaning began to appear in the early part of the new millennium, and they keep on coming. It is almost comic to read some authors who do quite a fancy dance of grappling with the obscure terminology and various distinctions that appear in the vast literature. I will consider here a sampling of some with pertinence to liturgy.

Jesuit Father Keith F. Pecklers, professor of liturgy at the Pontifical Gregorian University and professor of liturgical history at the Pontifical Liturgical Institute of Sant'Anselmo, Rome, uses the distinction between modern and postmodern movements in art, architecture and theater as a doorway into a discussion of cultural challenges and the future of authentic Christian worship.[6] He writes: "The world of postmodernism could be characterized—at least according to some scholars—as pessimistic, holistic, communitarian, and pluralistic."[7] Pessimism underscores human weakness and holds human progress suspect. Holism rejects rationality and privileges the emotions and intuitions. Communitarianism keeps in balance modernity's inclination to individualism in its search for communal truth. Pluralism encourages the diversity of cultural traditions and the necessity of various truths representing various communities. Pecklers describes the postmodern world as a place where "there is no one truth, no

---

[6] Keith F. Pecklers, S.J., *Worship: A Primer in Christian Ritual* (Collegeville, MN: Liturgical Press, 2003), 193-212.

[7] Pecklers, *Worship: A Primer in Christian Ritual*, 194.

one objective reality, no one way of negotiating life in the real world. Rather, the world is a complex symbol system that relies more on subjective interpretation than on absolute and demonstrable truth."[8] He then proceeds, in my judgment, with a rather apparent and obvious application of his description of postmodernism to pastoral circumstances with no prescriptive recommendations to solve the problems it poses.

Under another cover, Pecklers edited a collection of papers given at that Jesuit symposium on the liturgy in Rome in June 2002 that I mentioned earlier. Its title was *Liturgy in a Postmodern World*. Of the thirteen articles, only four have the word postmodern in the title. Nowhere can I find a hard attempt at a definition of the term. The closest I can find is in Peckler's introduction where he states: "The term 'post-Christian' is often linked with 'postmodern' as the role of religion is relegated to something private and personal."[9]

More recently, at the annual meeting of the North American Academy of Liturgy in January 2005, a new seminar group was initiated that called itself "Liturgy and the Postmodern Dialogue." As in most academies of study, new seminar groups are formed when an ample caucus forms with interest in pursuing a particular topic as applied to liturgy and worship. Episcopal priest James W. Farwell, assistant professor in the H. Boone Porter Chair of Liturgics at The General Theological Seminary, New York City, convened the seminar and wrote the summary for the academy's annual *Proceedings*.[10] Toying with philosophical and cultural dimensions to the meaning of "postmodernism," he sets out possible lines of inquiry when liturgy and postmodernism enter into dialogue with one another.[11] He proceeds by writing himself into a corner of such obscure density that I wonder if even his seminar colleagues had a clue as to what he was trying to get at.

Marist Father Gerald A. Arbuckle, now the co-director of the Refounding and Pastoral Research Unit in Sydney, Australia, has recently pressed beyond the postmodern to what he calls the "paramodern" in his effort to examine the phenomena of violence, power and culture, and their interplay. The "paramodern" is characterized by interde-

---

[8] Pecklers, *Worship: A Primer in Christian Ritual*, 194-195.

[9] Pecklers, *Liturgy in a Postmodern World*, 1-2.

[10] See James W. Farwell, "The Study of Liturgy and Postmodernism: Conceptual Maps and Possible Lines of Inquiry," *Proceedings of the North American Academy of Liturgy* (6-9 January 2005): 85-99.

[11] Farwell, 91-96.

pendence, collaboration, nonviolence, otherness, reconciliation, hope, freely chosen relationships, interconnected processes, and discerning patterns in chaos and sin, both social and ecological, where intuition and rationality interact.[12]

Still another addition to the ever-expanding nomenclature was suggested at an interdisciplinary seminar held at Calvin College in Grand Rapids, Michigan, in the summer of 2001. The seminar was titled "Loss of the Self in a Postmodern Therapeutic Culture." Only recently have the papers been published at the editorial hands of Paul Vitz, Professor Emeritus of Psychology at New York University, and Susan Felch, Professor of English at Calvin College, under the revised title, *The Self: Beyond the Postmodern Crisis*.[13] To describe what is "beyond," some authors use the term "transmodern," which Vitz defines in his introduction:

> Transmodern means a new understanding that *transforms* the modern and also *transcends* it [his emphasis]. This new approach does not reject modern contributions but transforms their meaning. Moreover, the new meaning is often a higher, transcendent nature—sometimes explicitly theological or spiritual but always with an emphasis on higher meaning.[14]

The most helpful for our purposes is the current contribution of Father R. Kevin Seasoltz, O.S.B., of St. John's Abbey, Collegeville, Minnesota. Seasoltz has been general editor of *Worship* for almost twenty years and was a former professor at The Catholic University of America and *mein Doktorvater*. In the first chapter of his book,[15] he delineates three categories of postmodern theology, each with a different commitment to premodern theology and philosophy: 1) deconstructionist (Jacques Derrida, John Caputo); 2) radical orthodoxy (Catherine Pickstock, Stanley Hauerwas); and 3) he assigns no name or tag but points to the representative figure of Jean-Luc Marion, who put clas-

---

[12] See Gerald A. Arbuckle, S.M., *Violence, Society, and the Church: A Cultural Approach* (Collegeville, MN: Liturgical Press, 2004), 29-31 and 215-239.

[13] *The Self: Beyond the Postmodern Crisis*, ed. Paul C. Vitz and Susan M. Felch (Wilmington, DE: ISI Books, 2006).

[14] Vitz and Felch, xviii.

[15] R. Kevin Seasoltz, O.S.B., *A Sense of the Sacred: Theological Foundations of Christian Architecture and Art* (New York: Continuum, 2005), 1-34.

sical negative theology in dialogue with post-Heideggerian phenomenology.[16]

> Three themes dominate [Marion's] work: idolatry, the gift, and love. He explores ways of thinking about God as beyond being. Especially important is his distinction between idol and icon. An idol is something that simply reflects our own gaze, whereas an icon points our sight beyond ourselves to something we cannot master. The ultimate icon is Christ, who intervenes in person in the celebration of the eucharist.[17]

Perhaps the tag on this third category could be "paramodern" or "transmodern." Seasoltz steps back from Marion's insights and continues to describe the postmodern as "dominated by the media" and "characterized by eclecticism and the exaltation of the popular and the occasional."[18] Postmodern culture is "in some ways a return to primal culture, to nature, to the images of good and evil, and to symbols, myths, and rituals that are thought to enable people not only to deal responsibly with the mystery of iniquity in human life but to triumph over that evil."[19] Postmodernism is "aware that the human person is a relational being existing with an orientation toward others and within a complex of traditions."[20] A certain strain of postmodern interpreters are "nihilistic in nature.... Others are more optimistic."[21] He continues to examine this second more optimistic strain, which, I believe, is important for our project here:

> Those who are rooted in the Christian tradition assert that human hope is grounded not ultimately in human achievements but rather in the power of the God who in Jesus Christ has conquered evil and has promised to save the world in Christ and through the power of the Holy Spirit. This renewed trust in divine providence accompanies an effort to deconstruct the modern conviction that the human person is a self-determined, autonomous being who has no need for religion or tradition; it posits that the human person is really a network

---

[16] Seasoltz, 29.
[17] Seasoltz, 29.
[18] Seasoltz, 29-30.
[19] Seasoltz, 30.
[20] Seasoltz, 30.
[21] Seasoltz, 30.

of relationships dependent ultimately on God but immediately dependent on community and traditions.[22]

These words do not exhaust Seasoltz's description of the postmodern. His explanation of Jean-Luc Marion's insights suggests something of Arbuckle's "paramodern" and of Paul Vitz's "transmodern," and thus help to broaden our scope, to widen our lense. We press on, then, in our project with the given that popular religious devotions could easily play into the dark side of the postmodern, i.e., the private, the personal, the individual, the self-absorbed, the pessimistic. We do not want our Franciscan devotions to get stuck there. We press on in our project also with the hunch that something within the tradition could in fact drive us out and up—out of what is private, personal, individual, self-absorbed, pessimistic and up into what is interdependent, collaborative, nonviolent, other-centered and reconciling. These could signal transcendence and hope. They may help us in our retrieval of Franciscan devotions for the next generation.

Franciscan Devotions

And it seems that it is just that, viz., for the next generation, if at all. Some devotions that I will examine are no longer intrinsic but extrinsic to us, i.e., we encourage them in the lives of the people we serve in our ministries, but they have curiously fallen through the cracks of our own Franciscan lives. My formation for this life has taken place in the last thirty-three years since first vows in 1973. In the decade after the Second Vatican Council, not only the Church but the entire world convulsed in change. My generation of friars—and I think many of us will testify to this truth, at least theoretically— was formed by formators who were largely in a state of intense reaction. The provincial administration and most (but not all) of the guardians and heads of the different levels of initial formation were "scraping away the layers of sediment" that had built up over the ages. I remember the metaphor so well. It seemed to be the right thing to do, listening to the "signs of the times." Then, the leveling of that sediment made way for the great onrush of the wave of Carl Rogers and the human potential movements that washed over us through the 1970s. And what a glorious time it was! In hindsight—and from a mid-life viewpoint—it has been diagnosed by some as a subtle form of

---

[22] Seasoltz, 30-31.

crypto-semi-Pelagianism, i.e., the sure, though not always conscious, conviction that humanity could save itself, as long as we "had a friend in Jesus."

To some ears, no doubt, that comment may sound rather cynical. But in reality, it is not far from the truth of what happened when it comes to devotions. Few Franciscan devotions survived the liturgical undertow after the reforms of the Council. By Franciscan devotions, I mean religious exercises whose texts and rubrics are contained neither in the official liturgical books of the Roman Church nor of the Seraphic Order. It is impossible to consider here all the devotions characterized as Franciscan. I choose four: 1) the Transitus, 2) the Stations of the Cross, 3) the Franciscan Crown and 4) St. Anthony Devotions.

Transitus

Memories of the Transitus linger from my first exposure to the rite as a seraphic seminarian. It was the evening of 3 October 1964. The Roman Church was rumbling in the second half of the Second Vatican Council. I was one month short of fourteen years of age, a baby who should have been home with his family, some would say. But it was a different world then. At least some of my sixty-four freshmen high school classmates and myself were awestruck by the simplicity of this rite. Suited up in black suit, white shirt and black tie, we sang the antiphon (*O sanctissima anima*), the psalm (142—*Voce mea ad Dominum clamavi*) and the hymn (*Salve, Sancte Pater*). At least some of the texts were rendered in the vernacular; it was quite the buzz in 1964.

But what lingers most in my memory are not the texts but the actions, the movements. As teenagers we were amused when the friars reached down to unbuckle their sandal straps and moved in a procession two-by-two toward the guardian who held the relic of St. Francis. On the approach, one by one, each friar genuflected three times before venerating the relic with a kiss. Not only were we amused by the power of this procession. We were amazed at the friars and inspired by their devotion and reverence. I was not the only one who, in my young mind and heart, said to himself: "I want to be one of them someday." We were being initiated into a culture, the Franciscan culture. Only later did some of us make the connection that this rite of passage from death to life imitated another rite of passage, the one we observed in those preconciliar days on Good Friday with a similar barefoot procession with its threefold genuflection prior to the veneration of the crucifix with a kiss.

Since those early days of pre-novitiate formation, the Transitus has always intrigued me, so much so that I began a collection. As time moved on, filing away mimeographed, purple-ditoed and "gestetner-ed" copies of postconciliar rituals became a kind of hobby. Other friars and sisters would send me their "liturgy aids," sometimes with commentary, to add to my collection. At twenty-five years of age, at the time of solemn profession, I probably had in my possession the largest collection of Transitus rituals in the world. As the years in initial formation passed, the discipline of theological studies generated questions and piqued my interest. Further graduate work in liturgical studies provided tools for ritual analysis, i.e., for theological reflection on ritual texts and actions and their interactions. Almost twenty years of active participation in Transitus rituals raised more questions for me—What did we think we were doing when we did this rite? What were we actually doing? What was it doing to us?

During doctoral studies, the rigor of directed reading courses, research projects and the production of research papers pressed me to make sense of my collection of rites that stretched from the late 1960s through the 1970s and into the early 1980s, rough-and-tumble years of reform and renewal in the Church, in American society and in the various North American Franciscan cultures. I was driven to examine the origin of the rite (late seventeenth and early eighteenth centuries), to examine the evolution of developing rites and, based on discernable patterns, to speculate about the future. Correspondence with some great twentieth-century Franciscan scholars thrilled me: Ignatius Brady, O.F.M., Octavian Schmucki, O.F.M. Cap., (who responded only in lengthy Latin letters), Dominic Unger, O.F.M. Cap., Peter Feltner, O.F.M. Conv., as well as the younger generation of budding scholars, Regis Armstrong, O.F.M. Cap., and Conrad Harkins, O.F.M. All of these letters I still hold and cherish. The results of my study were published in *The Cord* in three parts under the title, "The Transitus: A Rite of Intensification."[23]

The clutter of Transitus rites, especially through the 1970s and even into this new millennium, suggests to me confusion and conflict in our Franciscan identities. This rite, which is rightly "devotional" since it appears nowhere in official liturgical books, remains, while

---

[23] Part I, *The Cord* 43.10 (1993): 261-274; Part II, *The Cord* 43.12 (1993): 335-347; Part III, *The Cord* 44.3 (1994): 85-96. Unfortunately, the editors chose to eliminate the scholarly apparatus from the text, judging that the readers were not interested. Part I is available online at www.franciscanfriarstor.com/stfrancis/Transitus/index.htm thanks to the Friars of the Third Order Regular, Hollidaysburg, Pennsylvania.

most other Franciscan devotions perished in postconciliar Franciscan practice. Local communities entered into the struggle of sorting out who they were and who they wanted to become. My conclusion in the Transitus study was that it was one of the few devotional practices that allowed postconciliar Franciscans to work out ritual responses to perplexing questions. So they had unwittingly taken this rite, celebrated but once a year, and freighted it with almost everything that carries meaning for the Franciscan community. It mushroomed and mutated to rites within rites. Rituals turned into pantomime, and we all know, at least intuitively, that pantomime is not ritual.

My concluding recommendation was rather blunt and direct: Cut out the fat. Hardly a postmodern insight! Cut out the fat and reconstruct it close to its original lean lines: an appropriate hymn, the retelling of the story, the proclamation of John 13:1-17, Psalm 142 ("With a loud voice, I cry to the Lord"), a brief homily, a prayer of the faithful, the Our Father, a closing prayer, and a final blessing. Hardly an unfamiliar frame—and not too heavily freighted. Nevertheless, it is a ritual frame still supple and pliant enough to carry a variety of expressions as well as a variety of meanings.

This 3 October 2006 marks my forty-second celebration of the Transitus since that first encounter in 1964. Even to this day, the Transitus still intrigues me. Each year during the September liturgy preparation session, someone still asks (it never fails!): "What will be the theme of the Transitus this year?" Of course, the "theme" of the Transitus every year is "Francis dies." Plainly and simply that! And isn't that enough? The ritual choices we make still pique my ritual interests and sensibilities, but I must honestly say (and perhaps sad to say) that I have learned over the years to stay away from these preparation sessions. The rite still tends to grow, expand with layers and layers of fat. This is not to suggest that the rite ought to become rigid or fixed. That would be against our charism! The suppleness and pliancy of the rite ought to remain, while simplicity, balance and basic good taste prevail.

Still, whenever I see a habit, with tunic, cord and cowl lying on the floor in a swirling design with five candles to symbolize five wounds, the image simply refuses to take me to the Little Poor Man of Assisi. Rather, it takes me to Oz and the Wicked Witch of the West melting because of the water thrown on her. Careful distinctions must be made between healthy ritual development and expression and the horrors of liturgical bad taste. Wisdom figures in our community must speak up and call it what it is. Some ritual choices are downright tacky. Veteran Franciscans ought to step in, in all charity and courtesy, to tame youthful enthusiasms and challenge negligible artistic sensibilities that sometimes reside even in Franciscan souls.

As we continue to move into the twenty-first century, our rethinking of the Transitus as a powerful and meaning-laden rite of intensification demands ongoing and careful theological reflection. In this regard, perhaps we could learn something from our Eastern Christian brothers and sisters. The construct of their liturgical calendar does not permit them to celebrate a feast simply in one twenty-four hour period. No human being, they claim, can effectively celebrate a feast of significance solely in one day's time. It simply cannot be done. In order to provide a more intentional and purposeful ascent to and descent from the feast, they weave pre-festive and post-festive days directly into the liturgical calendar. Pre-festive days invite them to build up to the feast and post-festive days enable them to come down from the celebration. They actually call the days after the feast the "leave-taking" of this or that feast.

Could we not structure a similar movement for the annual celebration of the Solemnity of St. Francis? Perhaps its starting point would be the Feast of the Stigmata on 17 September. A kind of "house retreat" could begin on that day and be structured into the rhythm of the community's common prayer until 4 October and even thereafter. Likewise, pre-festive days for the Feast of St. Clare (11 August) could begin on the Feast of the Transfiguration (6 August) with leave-taking to the Feast of the Assumption (15 August).

Such a movement of preparation and leave-taking makes one think of the common practice for many communities and ministries in the celebration of "Francis Week." Its goal is to awaken the Franciscan tradition of the institution, whether a school or parish or an urban ministry site. Lecture series, discussions, movies and gatherings of all kinds enhance the actual celebration on 4 October and even extend it beyond that day. But these questions must be raised: Do we energetically attend to the liturgy, our life of common prayer, our common worship of God through Christ in the Spirit, at the time of such a festival? Do we attend to the liturgical leave-taking of the Solemnity? Or is 5 October just a day like any other?

Observing ritual ascent and descent could ease the strain on the Transitus ritual and on the feast day liturgy itself. The freight of this Solemnity, celebrated but once a year, might be more evenly distributed over a protracted span of time before and after the actual day, thus enabling fuller and more extensive formation of our Franciscan identities and reformation of our Franciscan communities. The Transitus would be, then, not idol, but icon.[24]

Stations of the Cross

As we saw earlier, the shape of the preconciliar Transitus rite echoed the Good Friday rite. Likewise, the Stations of the Cross grew organically from the memory of Francis's devotion to the Passion of the Lord. This popular devotion is practiced in our own day in the Latin Church, especially in the forty days of Lenten preparation for the Solemnity of the Resurrection. It consists in a ritual pilgrimage, moving from place to place, remembering the Lord with the help of images, prayers and hymns at fourteen spatially distanced representations of the sufferings of Christ on his way to Calvary. Each station or stop is a halting place where participants visit the moment of the Lord's suffering, contemplate its meaning and respond to the call to conversion. However, the fixed form of the Stations of the Cross as we know them today took some time to mature to fourteen specific and specified images. Francis and Clare, Bonaventure and Anthony would not have known this structure.

When the friars minor took on the care of the holy places in the Holy Land in 1342, they encouraged this ritual walk through the city streets to the mount of Calvary. Whether they themselves actually initiated the practice is not possible to establish with any degree of certainty. Pilgrims would travel by land and sea to walk what is now called the *Via Dolorosa* with hymns and prayers as they remembered Jesus' final journey to his execution.

While the rich could afford to make the once-in-a-lifetime pilgrimage to the Holy Land, the poor could not; and the poor, or those who were less than rich, constituted the majority of the medieval society. The genius of the friars was that they brought the Holy Land to the poor. They reconstructed the scenes as those who had actually made the pilgrimage remembered them, recreated the images, wrapped words and song and movement around them. The response was contagious, and a popular devotion was born. Or was it reborn? Traces of the Stations in a seminal form appear much earlier, even before the coming of the friars, well before Francis himself. In fact, the friars

---

[24] "An idol is something that simply reflects our own gaze, whereas an icon points our sight beyond ourselves to something we cannot master," to something that transcends itself. Cf., Seasoltz, 29.

probably experienced kindred practices as boys in Italy, well before they were missioned to serve in the Holy Land.

As early as the fifth century at the church of San Stefano in Bologna, Italy, there is evidence of the first coherently related "Stations" built outside Palestine, shrines with images depicting various moments in the Passion. Veterans of the Crusades erected various scenes representing the places they had visited in the Holy Land. There is testimony of shrines depicting as few as five and as many as forty images of different moments in the Passion.

Devotion to the Passion of Christ became widespread in the twelfth and thirteenth centuries, but it had not yet developed into depicting fourteen major moments along the way to Calvary. Throughout the fourteenth and fifteenth centuries, the practice of assembling a series of shrines commemorating places and events in the Passion continued. Popular prayer and preaching at these shrines found expression in devotion to the Stations of the Cross. From Franciscan churches and oratories, this devotion spread to parish churches throughout Western Europe. The potential for catechesis and evangelization is clear. In the eighteenth century, the popular preaching of Leonard of Port Maurice promoted the devotion so enthusiastically and successfully that he became known as "the preacher of the Way of the Cross." The Stations were set up in a variety of places—inside homes, outside homes in yards and gardens, inside churches, throughout the entire church or relegated to a section of the church.

The form of the Stations as fourteen specific units finally stabilized in 1731 in a *monitum* issued by Pope Clement XII. The fourteen are the same we use today.[25] After this *monitum* was issued, Leonard himself erected more than 572 sets of Stations until his death in 1751. The most important still stands very near the Colosseum on the steep road to San Buonaventura al Palatino where Leonard is buried. He also influenced the establishment of thousands of others throughout Europe and the expanding world.

I wonder what Leonard of Port Maurice would say to us today. As a boy, I prayed the Stations of the Cross and learned to sing the "Stabat

---

[25] Notice that not all are based in Scripture: 1) Pilate condemns Jesus to death; 2) Jesus is made to carry the cross; 3) Jesus falls the first time; 4) Jesus meets his mother Mary; 5) Simon of Cyrene is forced to carry the cross; 6) Veronica wipes the face of Jesus; 7) Jesus falls the second time; 8) Jesus speaks to the women of Jerusalem; 9) Jesus falls the third time; 10) Jesus is stripped of his garments; 11) Jesus is nailed to the cross; 12) Jesus dies on the cross; 13) Jesus is taken down from the cross; 14) Jesus is laid in the tomb of Joseph of Arimethea.

Mater." Later, as seraphic seminarians in high school, we prayed the Stations privately, walking around the chapel from one to the next, quietly on our own in the wee hours of the morning before 6:30 Mass. Only at the twelfth station did we kneel and do the "cross prayer," if only for a few seconds, self-conscious adolescents that we were. Later, as we rolled into the 1970s, the practice not only fell off but it crashed. Never were we encouraged, to my recollection, through novitiate and theological studies, to pray the Stations. There was no hostility against them, just no encouragement for them. Later on, returning to my province's post-novitiate house of formation as a professor at Washington Theological Union, students who inquired about the Stations were encouraged, I think wisely, to join the parish next door on Lenten Friday evenings.

What we have here in the Stations of the Cross is a guided meditation—Clement XII's version from 1731 and John Paul II's version from Good Friday 1991. At the Colosseum, John Paul recast this time-honored sequence of fourteen movements. Some claim the prefect of the Congregation on the Doctrine of the Faith, Joseph Cardinal Ratzinger, actually conceived and composed them.[26] Should we Franciscans be upset with his (their?) bold adjustments to our time-honored tradition? I think not. All fourteen are scripturally based; all fourteen coincide with the Passion Narrative proclaimed on Palm Sunday and Good Friday. Perhaps these are "new and improved," although the images may have to be replaced to line up with the new titles.[27]

This type of guided meditation seems to be in vogue today among the most famous of spiritual gurus. We have guided meditations for almost everything, e.g., "to enter my pre-conscious 'in utero' state" and "a conversation with God and my mother before I was born." We have a guided meditation for "Me and My Inner Child." Why not a guided meditation on the last moments in the earthly life of our

---

[26] Notice that they are all scripturally based: 1) Jesus in the Garden of Gethsemane; 2) Jesus, Betrayed by Judas, is Arrested; 3) Jesus is Condemned by the Sanhedrin; 4) Jesus is Denied by Peter; 5) Jesus is Judged by Pilate; 6) Jesus is Scourged and Crowned with Thorns; 7) Jesus Bears the Cross; 8) Jesus is Helped by Simon the Cyrenian to Carry the Cross; 9) Jesus Meets the Women of Jerusalem; 10) Jesus is Crucified; 11) Jesus Promises His Kingdom to the Good Thief; 12) Jesus Speaks to His Mother and the Disciple; 13) Jesus Dies on the Cross; 14) Jesus is Placed in the Tomb. The entire text is available on the Vatican website.

[27] The traditional fourteen stations of Clement XII are followed in Benedict XVI's first public praying of them. See *Way of the Cross at the Colosseum, Good Friday 2005, Meditations and Prayers by Benedict XVI* (Boston: Pauline Books & Media, 2005). The text is also available on the Vatican website.

"Wonder-Counselor, God-Hero, . . . Prince of Peace" (Is. 9:5)? After all, isn't that precisely what we Franciscans do each year on the evening of 3 October at Transitus? Is it not a guided meditation on the last moments in the earthly life of our saint, our hero? If the Transitus, then, is not idol but icon, the Stations of the Cross also are not idols but icons.

Franciscan Crown / Seraphic Rosary / Seven Joys

Once again, we return to the seraphic seminary in the mid-1960s. Every evening after supper when the weather was clement, herds of seraphic students would gather outside to circumambulate the lake while reciting the Franciscan Crown, the Seven Joys of the Blessed Mother.[28] Luke Wadding, O.F.M., testifies to its existence for the first time in 1422. So, images or statues of Francis, Clare, Anthony, or Bonaventure wearing a "side Crown" are anachronistic. As we walked around the lake in the minor seminary, a senior seraphic student would lead us in praying "the Crown." Some professed friars would join us in the walk. Slowly, we were being socialized into Franciscan culture. With each Our Father, Hail Mary and Glory Be, we fingered the beads and dreamed of the day when we would wear the Crown on our side as friars. But in time, all of that changed. As novices in the early 1970s, we were instructed that the Crown was no longer part of the habit. Peer pressure dictated that few novices hung it from their cords. The few who did were suspect, perhaps too pious in their desire to don so-called "waist jewelry." In time, the operating principle emerged: "If you pray the Crown, you may wear it. If you don't, don't." Today, my hunch is that most don't, even though wearing it doesn't mean you do! In my own province, I know of no house that regularly or even sometimes gathers to pray the Crown communally. If at all, it has become a personal and private devotion among a very few.

At the same time, in our own day in the Roman Church, we are witnessing a revival of the private and communal praying of the traditional Dominican fifteen-decade Rosary—the Joyful Mysteries (Mondays and Saturdays), the Sorrowful Mysteries (Tuesdays and Fridays), the Glorious Mysteries (Wednesdays and Sundays), and the recent addition by Pope John Paul II of the Luminous Myster-

---

[28] The Seven Joys are the Annunciation, the Visitation, the Birth of the Lord, the Adoration of the Magi, the Finding of the Child Jesus in the Temple, the Resurrection of the Lord, the Assumption of Mary and her Coronation in Heaven.

ies (Thursdays). Although this revival is not growing by leaps and bounds, it is nonetheless significant in its increase, even beyond faithful viewers of E.W.T.N.

Cultural historian and Catholic author, Garry Wills, recently published a book entitled *The Rosary: Prayer Comes Round*.[29] He examines this regular round of prayer as a daily devotion, a guided meditation on events in the life of Jesus. While the Rosary is often categorized under Marian Devotion, eighteen of the twenty episodes for meditation are not about Mary but solely about her Son.[30] Most of the episodes, but not all, are revealed in Sacred Scripture. Popular devotion is giving rise to this renewed practice of a daily guided meditation on key moments in the life of the Lord.

Some of us may find this revival more than curious. Things get even more curious when we look to pop culture icons who often manipulate rosaries, swing them around, or wear them around their necks in their music videos. Lindsay Lohan prayed with them in a recent video and Madonna was now and then seen with a pair of rosaries in the 1980s and 1990s. It is commonplace now to see young people benecklaced with rosaries or hanging them on the rearview mirror of their cars.

However, it is not this kind of revival that I find curious. I am referring more directly to the response to a craving for spirituality, to a search for methods of prayer that will carry meanings and discoveries of Christ and of self. Parochial life witnesses to this craving and this search. Recently, I was amused by a Franciscan friend who was actually put out by people praying the Rosary aloud before a scheduled Mass. They were "a distraction to my prayer," she said. But popular piety and devotion is expressing itself in this way in many places, at least in the part of the world where I live, i.e., the northeastern part of this country.

Those connected to parochial life on a regular basis know that most parishes have a group of people who pray the Rosary, even every day, before or after Mass. Why would one be put out by this reality? My generation remembers the glory days of Carl Rogers and his friends in the 1960s and 1970s. Today's Catholics who stand left of center are the ones who say time and again that "we must meet people where they are." Hardly a postmodern insight! So, the reality of people publicly praying the Rosary is a given. What do we as Franciscans

---

[29] Garry Wills, *The Rosary: Prayer Comes Round* (New York: Viking, 2005).

[30] The two exceptions are the fourth and fifth Glorious Mysteries: the Assumption of Mary and her Coronation.

do with this reality? Forbid it? Condemn it? Remain indifferent to it? Or perhaps join in, at least now and then, and even give instructions in meditating on the Seven Joys of Mary that bespeak one of our often self-identified charisms, i.e., joy.

A few years ago in our post novitiate formation house, a small group of young friars requested the scheduling of the recitation of the Rosary in the friary chapel to encourage devotion to Christ through Mary. The guardian approved the request. A few weeks later, I was surprised to learn that the friar who was leading the practice was praying, not the Franciscan Crown, but the five decades of the Dominican Rosary with the hope of moving through all fifteen decades in a week's time. Throughout the entire house chapter discussion, I had been working on the assumption that the seven-decade Franciscan Rosary would be prayed. After all, Franciscans ought to do Franciscan things. It seemed only logical. I was saddened to learn that the friars who gathered for this devotion, all at least one year out of the novitiate, had never heard of the Franciscan Crown and were clueless about how to pray it.

Franciscans are known for meeting people where they are and accepting them there. If Franciscans have always evangelized and catechized people effectively by tapping into their imaginations and engaging them with tales and stories of meaning and value, could we not use these "Seven Joys" to extend that vital aspect of our charism? The great virtue of joy leaps off the page at us in those earliest stories of the brothers who lived with Francis. Perhaps, on second or third thought, praying the Seraphic Rosary, the Seven Joys of Mary, the Franciscan Crown, might be more trustworthy than we thought. Not an idol but an icon.

St. Anthony Novena / Shrines

Every Tuesday at St. Bonaventure Church in Paterson, New Jersey, people come to pray the traditional novena prayers to St. Anthony of Padua at the National Shrine of St. Anthony in the United States. Of course, friars always laugh at this statement because they know (and I suppose you do, too) that there are at least seven (or is it seventeen?) shrines that claim to be "the" National Shrine of St. Anthony. However, it can be proven historically that St. Anthony Shrine, Paterson, is the mother of all the shrines of St. Anthony, at least within the boundaries of Holy Name Province. All others are spawned from it.

In our church in Paterson, as in most places, there are devotions to St. Anthony every Tuesday of the year; but twice a year there are two special novenas: 1) nine Tuesdays before Christmas with a focus on the Incarnation and 2) thirteen Tuesdays before 13 June, the Feast of St. Anthony. There is one central novena prayer recited every Tuesday in unison. There are special proper prayers for each week of the Christmas novena and for each week of the feast-day novena. The prayer text of that one central novena prayer has been in use for a good long time. I confess that I cringe each time I pray it. I find it theologically reprehensible, even risible. Yet I continue to pray it because, if one attempted to change it, an upsurge of revolt would undoubtedly arise from the novena goers. And so, I take a hard swallow and pray the prayer. Some Franciscan churches have made text changes without incident. Just as "all theology is local," so too is pastoral ministry local.

For whatever reason, on the Tuesdays before Christmas and before 13 June, the church where I serve is filled with two to three hundred people—which is good for us! As I look at the faithful, my thoughts wander to five or ten years down the road. Who will still be there? Is this "Great Generation" that we are now burying the last generation of novena goers? Will we lose this devotion to St. Anthony? Or is it time for the devotion to die? Do we keep this devotion alive only because it still proves lucrative? Or could we retrieve the core of the Saint's preaching and popularize it again for a new generation by way of guided meditations? Could not these Tuesdays be an opportunity to highlight some of the great themes of Anthony's theology and preaching? The story goes that Anthony first came to be noticed among the friars as a popular and effective preacher when he was called on (or placed under obedience) to substitute on short notice for another preacher who could not fulfill his commitment. That story tells us that Anthony must have had something to say. Perhaps he still has something to say. Our generation may find ways to repackage Anthony's message and communicate it in our marketplaces.[31]

Michael Cusato, O.F.M., the current Director of the Franciscan Institute, thinks that "something's lost and must be found," to quote the prayer to Saint Anthony that most of us have known by heart since

---

[31] To assist in this effort, see George Marcil O.F.M., ed., *Anthony of Padua:* Sermones *for the Easter Cycle* (St. Bonaventure, NY: The Franciscan Institute, 1994).

we were children.[32] The Anthony of history "can speak to the spiritual vision of men and women of the twenty-first century who value integrity of life and an evangelical sense of justice."[33] The Anthony of history needs to be reclaimed in order for the Anthony of devotions to survive.

Ignatius Press recently published the first feature length dramatic film (95 minutes) on the life of St. Anthony. It is directed by Umberto Marino.[34] I am convinced that some of our most dedicated novena goers know little or nothing about the Saint's life and would profit from seeing this film. It is extremely well put together, with an engaging script and very good actors. Some "schmaltz," but every Italian film has a touch of the hopelessly romantic, some "opera"! Anthony wears around his neck a tau cross given to him at his reception into the brotherhood by Francis himself. A bit of anachronism but, nonetheless, effective in the story line, and it connects with young people today. Unfortunately, the film is subtitled, not dubbed, in English. While some novena goers have Italian as their first language, many cannot hear well and/or see well. So the movie might not be effective unless shown on a huge digital screen with a state-of-the-art sound system. (Something highly unlikely for my parish!)

But the film would be useful for friars and sisters, especially those in formation. It is likely that their exposure to this type of thing is next to nothing, and they rely on "on the job training" when they leave initial formation and step into the responsibilities of active ministry. Seeing this film may provide for any of us a way to retrieve the historical Anthony, whom Michael Cusato presents so well in his two articles.

In what other ways could that retrieval be done? Perhaps the thirteen meditations classically presented during the thirteen weeks of the novena before his feast day could be refurbished. They are: 1) pure intention; 2) death; 3) fight the devil; 4) work for eternal salvation; 5) watch and pray; 6) sin; 7) human life exposed to many dangers; 8) our passions; 9) St. Anthony helps his devotees; 10) St. Anthony's protection; 11) help the poor; 12) the Most Holy Trinity; 13) the name of Jesus.

---

[32] See his two-part article, "'Something's Lost and Must Be Found...': The Recovery of the Historical Anthony of Padua" (Part I), *The Cord* 52.2 (2002): 58-71, (Part II), *The Cord* 52.3 (2002): 106-113.

[33] Cusato, Part II, 112.

[34] *Saint Anthony: The Miracle Worker of Padua* (Ft. Collins, CO: Ignatius Press, 2003).

Granted, several of these items are negative (modern or even pre-modern), but could be easily juxtaposed with a positive aspect, e.g., death (and eternal life); fight the devil (and embrace Christ's light); sin (and grace); our passions (and our gifts), etc. These thirteen windows could open the minds and hearts of the friends of St. Anthony. They would be exposed to basic notions of Franciscan theology over a period of thirteen consecutive Tuesdays. At the end of the novena, they would know the Saint more deeply and maybe even absorb a better sense of what we are up to as Franciscans. The thirteen meditations would be not idols but icons.

Conclusion

What concluding comments can be made after thinking around these four Franciscan devotions? First, nothing in what I have said will actually solve the dilemmas that face us in our postmodern, paramodern and transmodern culture. I hope however, that what I have said could actually contribute to an ongoing discussion among us as sons and daughters of our Franciscan heritage. Most important of all, our devotions, whether expressed among us in our own oratories or among the Christian assembly in our various ministries, must always express and support the conviction that God is not only immanent in creation but transcendent as well. Never ought our devotions make an idol out of Francis, Anthony, or any other human embodiment of God's presence among us. They ought to be icons through which the God of Francis, Anthony and the rest is worshiped and glorified. To be authentically Franciscan, our devotions must challenge people to involve themselves in both the ongoing creation of the universe and the critical transformation of the world. And, finally, truly Franciscan devotions will both support and challenge people in their conviction that it is not humanity that ultimately saves the world and brings it to fulfillment, it is God—God alone in Jesus Christ through the power of the Holy Spirit.

AUTHORS

William Cieslak, O.F.M., Cap., is a liturgical theologian who served at the Franciscan School of Theology, Berkeley, California, from 1980 to 2004. For the last twelve of those years, he was President of the School. He also served as a visiting professor at the Institute of Spirituality and Theology, Old Mission, Santa Barbara, California, and at the Vatican II Institute, Menlo Park, California. Among his publications, he counts "Putting Heart into Liturgy," *Liturgy and Music: Lifetime Learning*, ed. Robin Leaver and Joyce Zimmerman (Collegeville: The Liturgical Press, 1998); "Putting Heart into Liturgy," *Liturgical Ministry* 1 (Spring 1992): 55-59; "Funeral Basics: a Practical Guide to the New Rite," in *Pastoral Music in Practice*, vol. 4, *Weddings, Funerals, Liturgy of the Hours,* ed. Virgil Funk (Washington, DC: The Pastoral Press, 1990), 69-74; *Console One Another: Commentary on The Order of Christian Funerals* (Washington, DC: The Pastoral Press, 1990). He currently lives in Chicago and works in development for his province.

Catherine Dooley, O.P., a member of the Dominican Sisters of Sinsinawa, Wisconsin, is professor of liturgy and catechetics at the School of Theology and Religious Studies, Catholic University of America, Washington, DC. She holds Master of Arts and Doctor of Philosophy degrees from the Catholic University of Louvain, Belgium. Her doctoral dissertation is *An Historical and Theological Study of Devotional Confession*. Recently, the Georgetown Center for Liturgy honored her with a National Award for Outstanding Contribution to the Liturgical Life of the American Church. She is author of *To Listen and Tell: Commentary on the Introduction to the Lectionary for Masses with Children* (Washington, DC: Pastoral Press, 1993) and co-editor of *The Echo Within: Emerging Issues in Religious Education* (Allen, TX: Thomas More, 1997). Currently, she is preparing to publish *Be What You Celebrate*, a work on liturgical catechesis.

Ilia Delio, O.S.F., a member of the Franciscan Servants, did her doctoral studies in theology at Fordham University. She is presently at Washington Theological Union, Washington, DC, serving as associate professor of ecclesial history and Franciscan studies and as Director of the Franciscan Center. She is author of *Crucified Love: Bonaventure's Mysticism of the Crucified Christ* (Quincy: Franciscan Press, 1998), *Simply Bonaventure: An Introduction to His Life, Thought, and Writings* (New York: New City Press, 2001) and *A Franciscan View of Creation: Learning to Live in a Sacramental World,* Vol. 2, The Franciscan Heritage Series (CFIT-ESC-OFM) (St. Bonaventure, NY: The Franciscan Institute, 2003).

Daniel P. Grigassy, O.F.M., a member of Holy Name Province, did his doctoral studies at the Catholic University of America. He served as assistant professor of liturgy at Christ the King Seminary, East Aurora, New York, and subsequently as associate professor of liturgy and sacrament and chair of the Word and Worship Department at Washington Theological Union (1991-2003). In 1993, he published a three-part article on the Transitus in *The Cord* (43.10, 43.12 and 44.3). The first two parts are available on the website of the Franciscan Friars Third Order Regular (franciscanfriarstor.com). In 2003, his article, "Is Roman the Only Way to be Catholic?: A Reflection of the Grandson of a Catholic Priest," appeared in *New Theology Review* and, in 2004, "The Eastern Catholic Churches in America," in *Contemporary Review,* a British journal. He is also a past resident scholar at The Metropolitan Andrey Sheptytsky Institute of Eastern Christian Studies, St. Paul University, Ottawa, Ontario, and at the Institute for Ecumenical and Cultural Research, St. John's University, Collegeville, Minnesota. At present, he is pastor of St. Bonaventure Church, Paterson, New Jersey.

Judith Marie Kubicki, C.S.S.F., holds a Doctor of Philosophy degree in Liturgical Studies from the School of Theology and Religious Studies, Catholic University of America, Washington, DC. She is presently assistant professor of sacramental and liturgical theology at Fordham University in New York. Before holding this position, she served as director of music, associate professor of theology and, later, as academic dean at Christ the King Seminary in East Aurora, New York. In 2001, she received the Sister/Brotherhood Award for Outstanding Leadership in Promoting Goodwill and Understanding in the Community through Interfaith Dialogue, presented by the National Conference for Community and Justice, Buffalo, New York. A prolific writer, she is author of *The Presence of Christ in the Gathered Assembly* (New York: Continuum, 2006) and *Liturgical Music as Ritual Symbol: A Case Study of Jacques Berthier's Taizé Music* (Leuven: Peeters

Publishers, 1999). Her articles have appeared in such notable journals as *America, Studia Liturgica, Theological Studies* and *Worship.*

James G. Sabak, O.F.M., is a member of Holy Name Province, New York, and is currently a third year doctoral student in the School of Theology and Religious Studies, Catholic University of America, with a concentration in Sacramental Theology and Liturgy. He was a teaching fellow at the School of Theology and Religious Studies in fall 2005, during which time he designed and taught a course on the evolution, historical significance and contemporary consequences of the social teachings of the Catholic Church. From 1997-1998, he was a lecturer at Siena College, Albany, New York, where he designed and taught a course in the theology behind and historical evolution of sacramental practices and understandings in the Catholic Church and a course in Christology.